GIRL GENIUS

AGATHA HETERODYNE
& THE
CIRCUS OF DREAMS

A Gaslamp Fantasy
with
ADVENTURE, ROMANCE & MAD SCIENCE

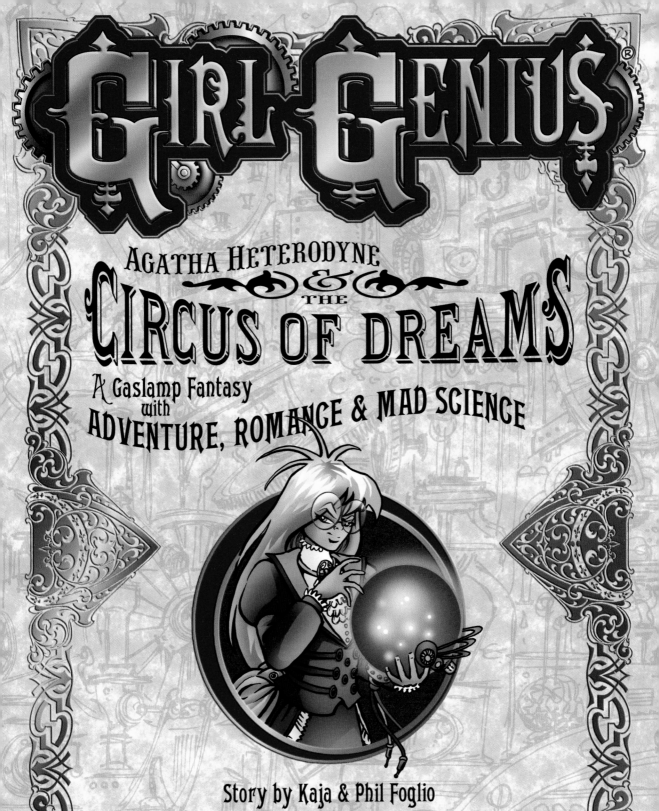

Story by Kaja & Phil Foglio
Pencils by Phil Foglio
Colors by Laurie E. Sm

AIRSHIP ENTERTAINMENT

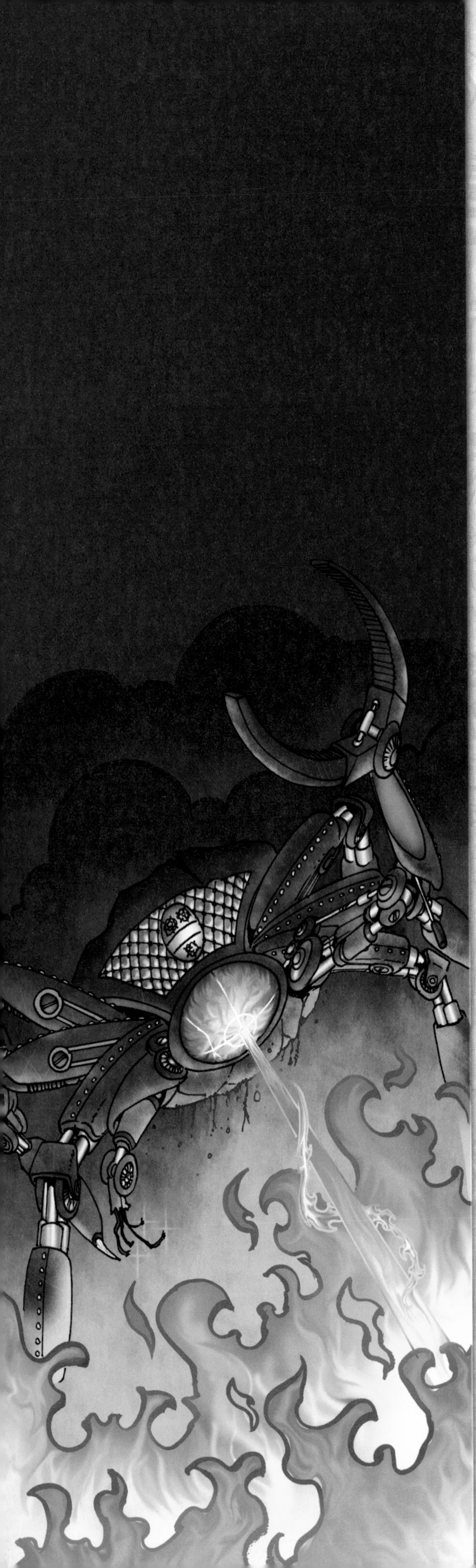

OTHER BOOKS FROM AIRSHIP ENTERTAINMENT AND STUDIO FOGLIO

Girl Genius® Graphic Novels

Girl Genius Volume One:
Agatha Heterodyne and the Beetleburg Clank

Girl Genius Volume Two:
Agatha Heterodyne and the Airship City

Girl Genius Volume Three:
Agatha Heterodyne and the Monster Engine

Girl Genius Volume Four:
Agatha Heterodyne and the Circus of Dreams

Girl Genius Volume Five:
Agatha Heterodyne and the Clockwork Princess

Girl Genius Volume Six:
Agatha Heterodyne and the Golden Trilobite

Girl Genius Volume Seven:
Agatha Heterodyne and the Voice of the Castle

Girl Genius Volume Eight:
Agatha Heterodyne and the Chapel of Bones

Other Graphic Novels

What's New with Phil & Dixie Vol.s 1-3

Robert Asprin's MythAdventures®

Buck Godot, zap gun for hire:
- *Three Short Stories*
- *PSmIth*
- *The Gallimaufry*

Girl Genius® is published by:
Airship Entertainment™, a happy part of Studio Foglio, LLC
2400 NW 80th St #129 Seattle WA 98117-4449, USA

Please visit our Web sites at www.airshipbooks.com and www.girlgeniusonline.com

Story by Phil & Kaja Foglio. Pencils by Phil Foglio. Main story colors by Laurie E. Smith. *Fan Fiction* written by Shaenon K. Garrity, with colors by Cheyenne Wright. Selected spot illos colored by Kaja Foglio and Cheyenne Wright. Logos, Lettering, Artist Bullying & Book Design by Kaja. Fonts mostly by Comicraft– www.comicbookfonts.com.

Much of the material in this collection was originally published in the Girl Genius comic book issues 10-13. The rest appeared three times a week at girlgeniusonline.com April-June 2005.

Softcover Edition: ISBN #978-1-890856-22-9

Third Printing: May 2009 PRINTED IN THE USA

This book is dedicated to Marie Cooley and Payne Fifield, who are even more amazing than their cartoon avatars.

Phil Foglio

Professor Foglio specializes in field research. His latest paper concludes that most of them are rectangular and need weeding. He is also an expert in the early life of Agatha Heterodyne, and is the author of the much-admired Jägermonster/Romanian dictionary and phrase book, "Hey Dere, Sveethøt." He has vowed to remain in the field until he can find his keys.

Kaja Foglio

Professor Foglio had the satisfaction of seeing her last paper chronicling the life of Agatha Heterodyne read aloud before the Academy of Letters and Egregious Punctuation for unprecedented mastery of the semi-colon. Disaster was narrowly averted earlier this year, when a newly refurbished Mr. Tock inexplicably attempted to hunt her down and step on her, doing quite a bit of damage to the campus of Transylvania Polygnostic before she was able to lure it out onto the then-frozen surface of Tozer-Kilts Pond. Baffled university engineers expressed amazement at "—how fast she could run in those shoes."

Laurie E. Smith

Continuing her experiments with blasphemous color theory, Professor Smith was the person responsible for turning the entire sky orange for several days last year—an incident noticed by surprisingly few people. She plans to continue her research until she finds a color she likes.

Shaenon K. Garrity

Professor Garrity is known primarily for her own researches. These chronicle the life of girl mad scientist Helen Narbon, who inhabits a fascinating parallel world *quite different* from our own. Professor Garrity meticulously creates a new chapter of her chronicle every day, then electrifies it and claims that it spreads across the entire world via wires and glass. Sure. We will concede, however, that interesting results have been obtained by having our electro-mechanical Ouija boards spell out the mysterious phrase "www.narbonic.com"

Cheyenne Wright

Professor Wright was found emerging from a cave beneath Transylvania Polygnostic University several years ago, dressed in an outfit made from the skins of several hundred bats. The University Board, a cowardly and superstitious lot, immediately gave him tenure if he would only promise to stop "looking at them like that." He has been routinely mocked for his assertions that colors are composed entirely of numbers, but is greatly admired by the student body for his fashion sense. You can view the latest results of his work at www.arcanetimes.com.

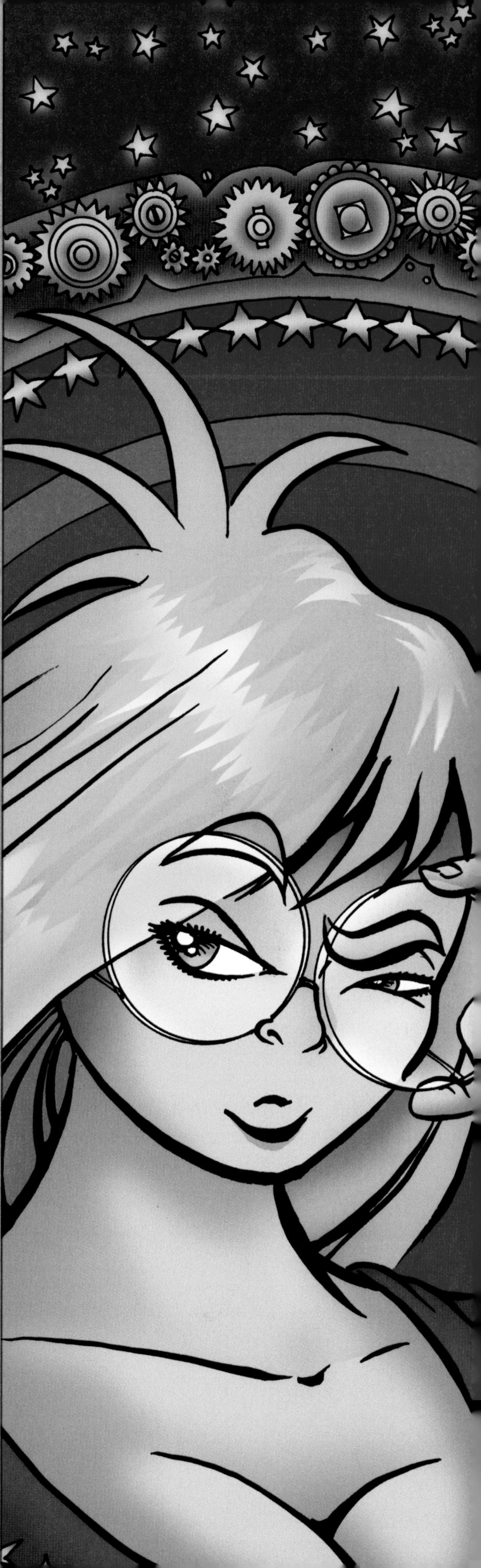

OUR STORY THUS FAR

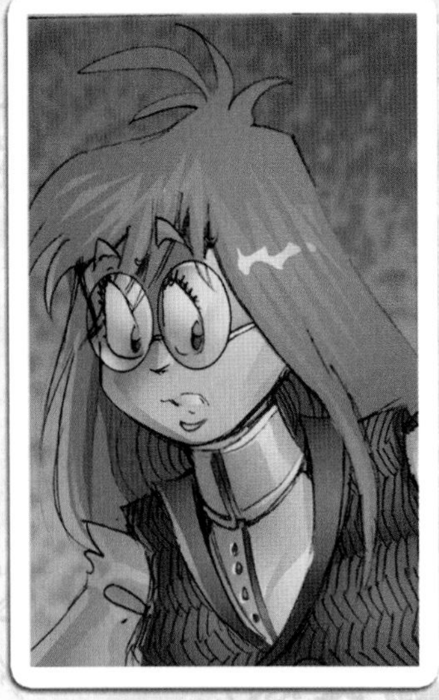

Agatha Clay is a Spark—capable of scientific wonders.
She has recently discovered that she is also the last of the famous Heterodyne family—

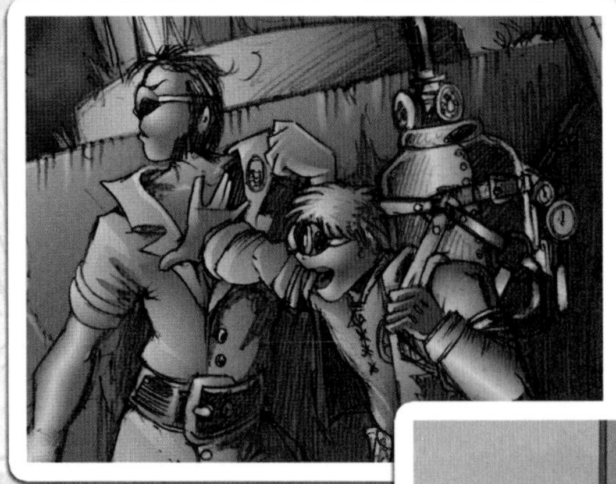

—heroes who disappeared mysteriously many years ago.

Folk legend claims they will someday return.

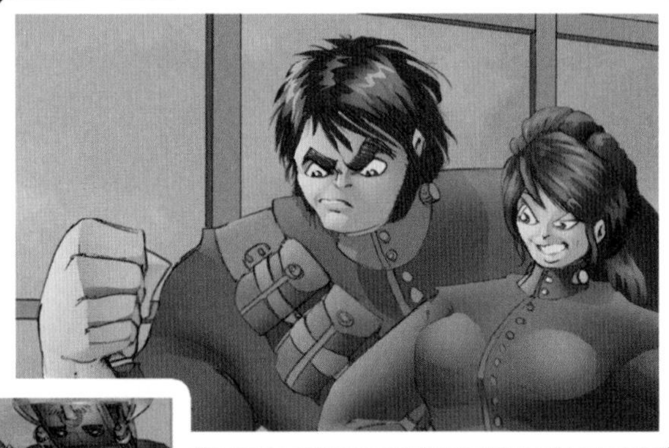

Agatha was raised by **Adam and Lilith Clay**—
a pair of constructs built by her father and uncle.
Adam & Lilith are better known in stories of the Heterodynes as Punch and Judy.
The Clays have just helped Agatha escape from the giant airship Castle Wulfenbach; at the cost of their lives.

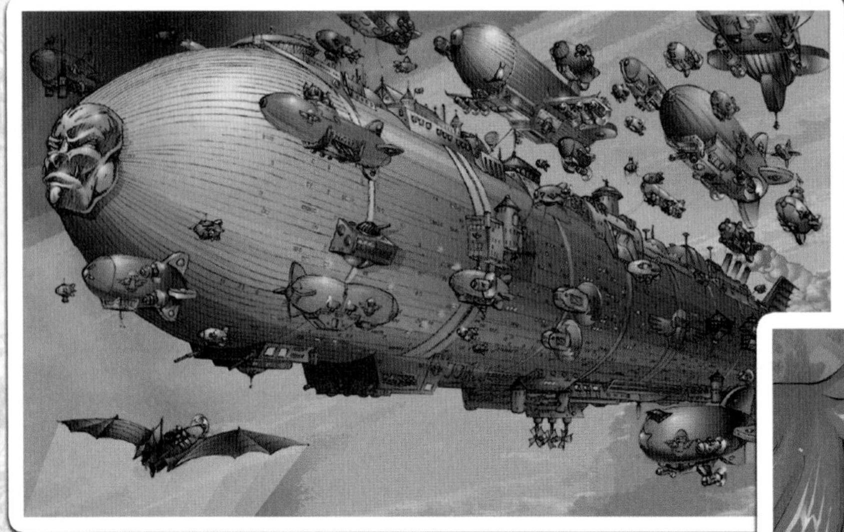

Also fleeing the Castle is Krosp—a failed experiment created to be the King of the Cats.

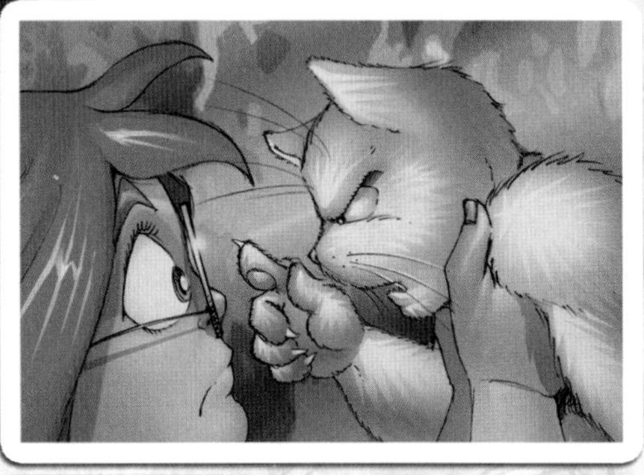

Castle Wulfenbach is the fortress of **Baron Klaus Wulfenbach**—
an old companion of the Heterodynes who now rules Europe with an iron fist.
The Baron would prefer to keep Agatha safely a prisoner.

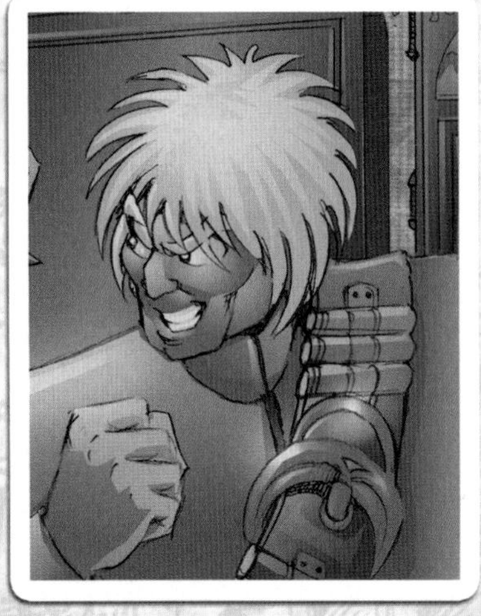

The Baron's son Gilgamesh would also like her to stay, but he has other reasons.

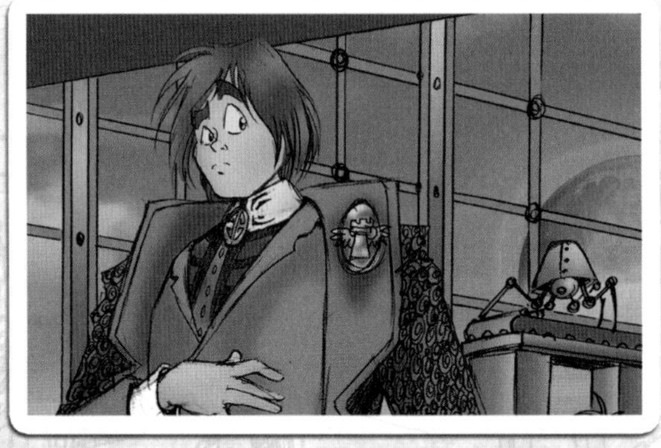

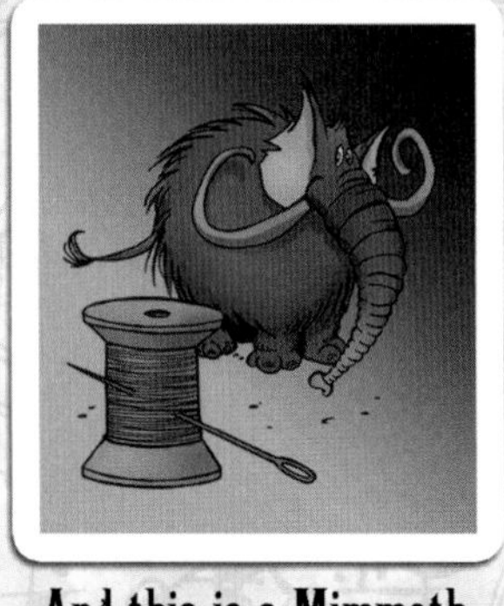

And this is a Mimmoth.

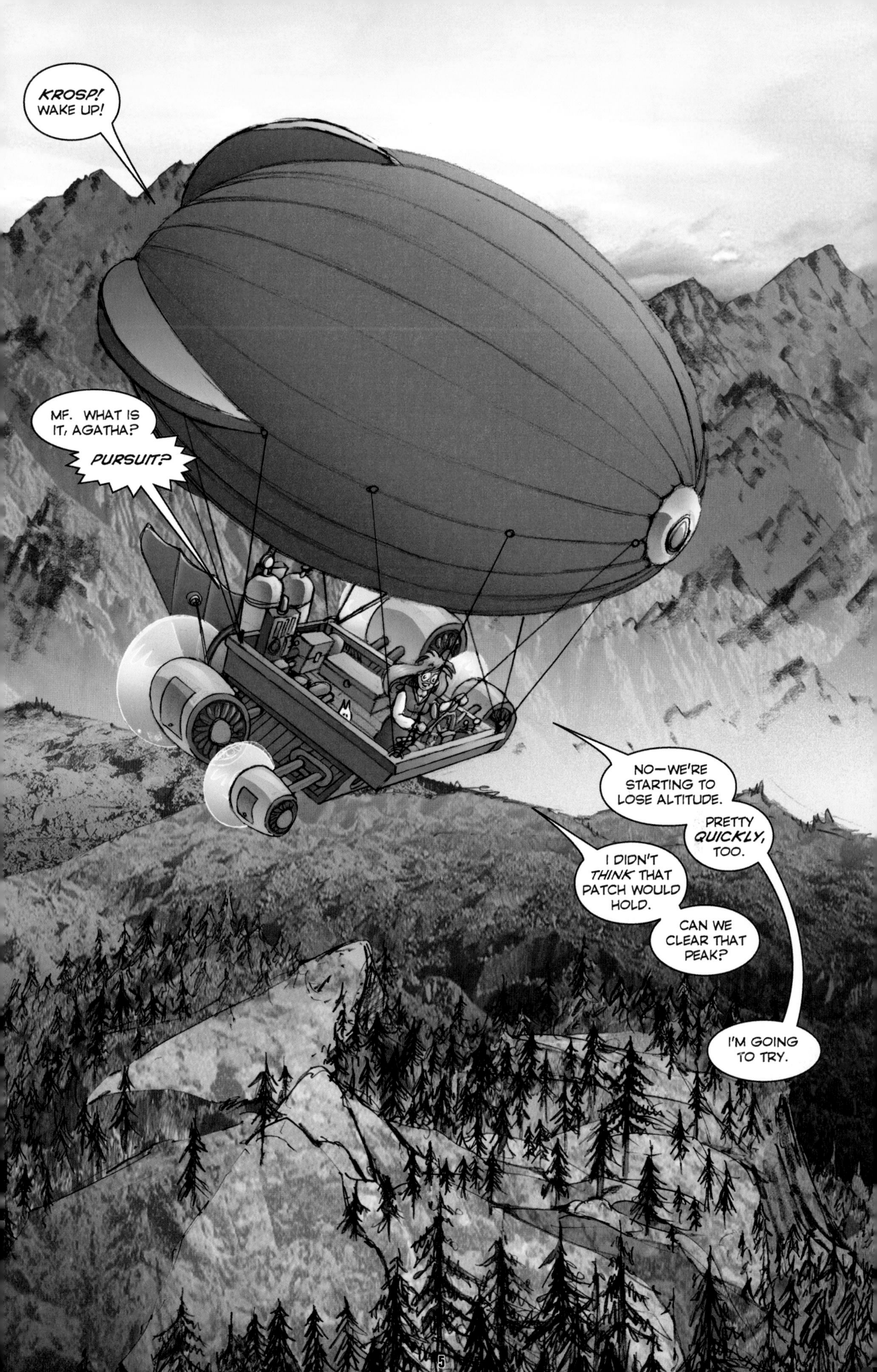
KROSP! WAKE UP!
MF. WHAT IS IT, AGATHA?
PURSUIT?
NO—WE'RE STARTING TO LOSE ALTITUDE.
PRETTY QUICKLY, TOO.
I DIDN'T THINK THAT PATCH WOULD HOLD.
CAN WE CLEAR THAT PEAK?
I'M GOING TO TRY.

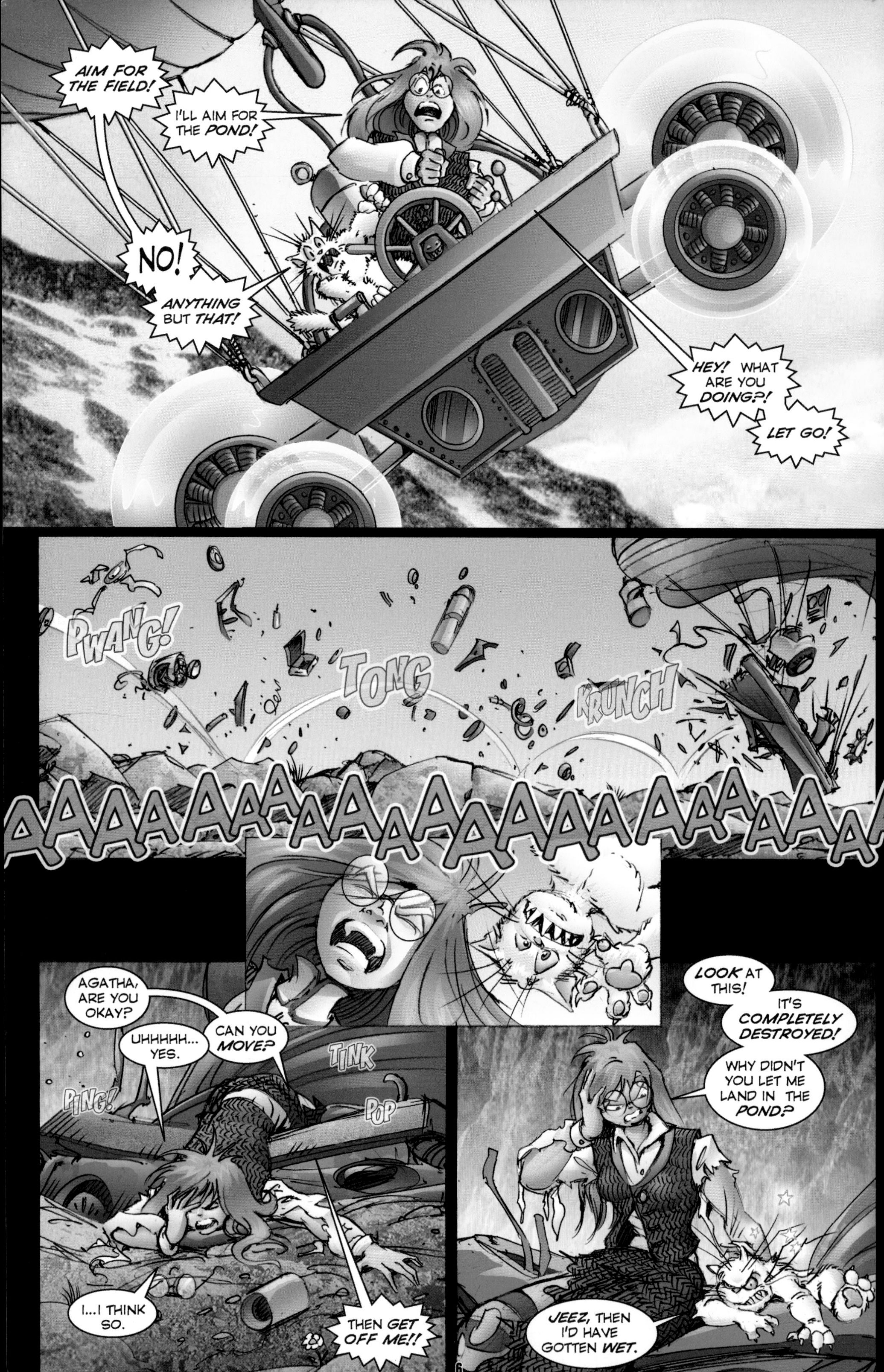
AIM FOR THE FIELD!
I'LL AIM FOR THE POND!
NO!
ANYTHING BUT THAT!
HEY! WHAT ARE YOU DOING?!
LET GO!
PWANG!
TONG
KRUNCH
AAAAAAAAAAAAAAAAAAAAAA
AGATHA, ARE YOU OKAY?
UHHHHH... YES.
CAN YOU MOVE?
TINK
PING!
POP
I...I THINK SO.
THEN GET OFF ME!!
LOOK AT THIS!
IT'S COMPLETELY DESTROYED!
WHY DIDN'T YOU LET ME LAND IN THE POND?
JEEZ, THEN I'D HAVE GOTTEN WET.

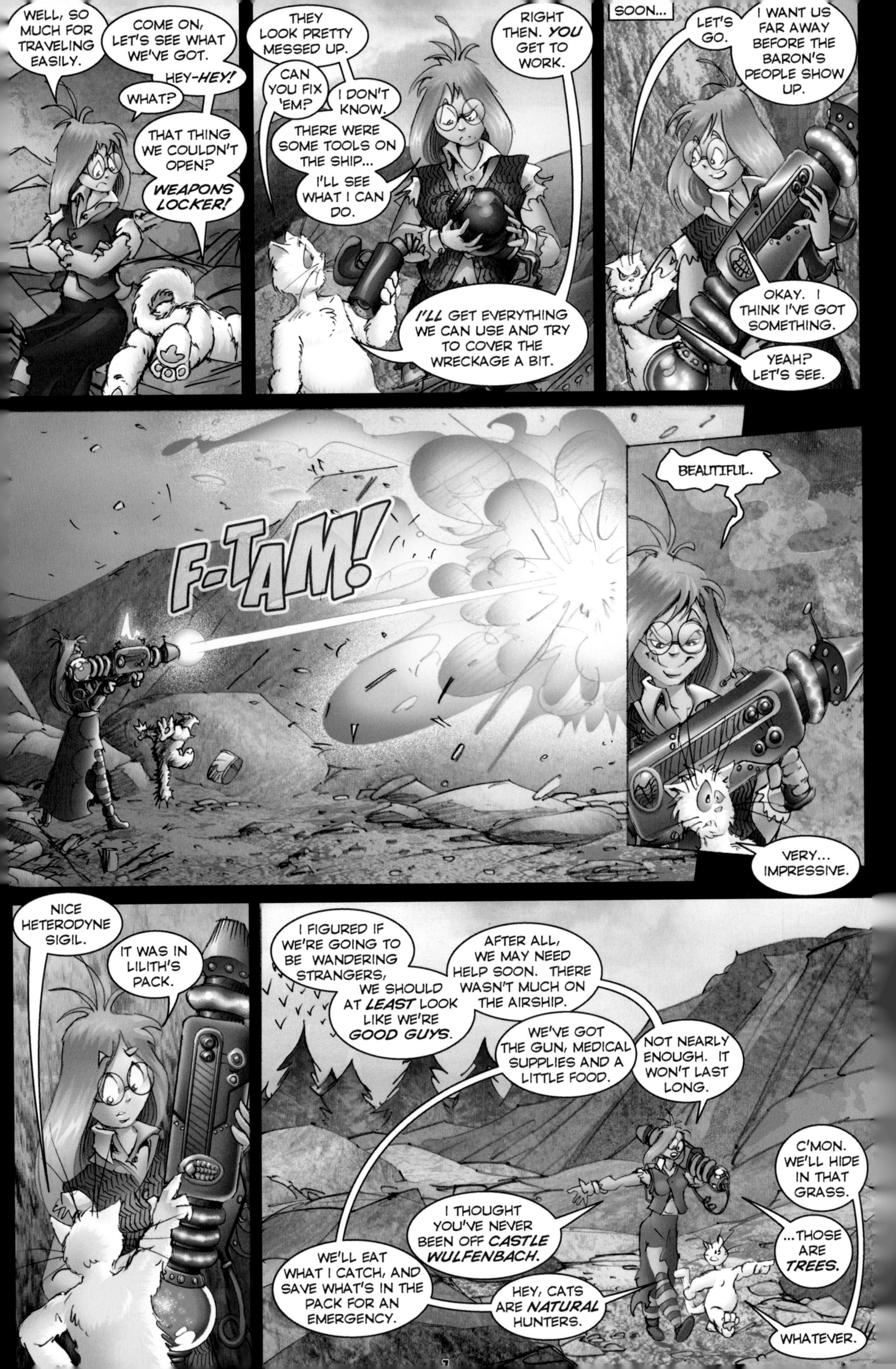
WELL, SO MUCH FOR TRAVELING EASILY.
COME ON, LET'S SEE WHAT WE'VE GOT.
HEY-*HEY!*
WHAT?
THAT THING WE COULDN'T OPEN?
WEAPONS LOCKER!
THEY LOOK PRETTY MESSED UP.
CAN YOU FIX 'EM?
I DON'T KNOW.
THERE WERE SOME TOOLS ON THE SHIP...
I'LL SEE WHAT I CAN DO.
RIGHT THEN. *YOU* GET TO WORK.
I'LL GET EVERYTHING WE CAN USE AND TRY TO COVER THE WRECKAGE A BIT.
SOON...
LET'S GO.
I WANT US FAR AWAY BEFORE THE BARON'S PEOPLE SHOW UP.
OKAY. I THINK I'VE GOT SOMETHING.
YEAH? LET'S SEE.
F-TAM!
BEAUTIFUL.
VERY... IMPRESSIVE.
NICE HETERODYNE SIGIL.
IT WAS IN LILITH'S PACK.
I FIGURED IF WE'RE GOING TO BE WANDERING STRANGERS, WE SHOULD AT *LEAST* LOOK LIKE WE'RE *GOOD GUYS*.
AFTER ALL, WE MAY NEED HELP SOON. THERE WASN'T MUCH ON THE AIRSHIP.
WE'VE GOT THE GUN, MEDICAL SUPPLIES AND A LITTLE FOOD.
NOT NEARLY ENOUGH. IT WON'T LAST LONG.
WE'LL EAT WHAT I CATCH, AND SAVE WHAT'S IN THE PACK FOR AN EMERGENCY.
I THOUGHT YOU'VE NEVER BEEN OFF *CASTLE WULFENBACH*.
HEY, CATS ARE *NATURAL* HUNTERS.
C'MON. WE'LL HIDE IN THAT GRASS.
...THOSE ARE *TREES.*
WHATEVER.

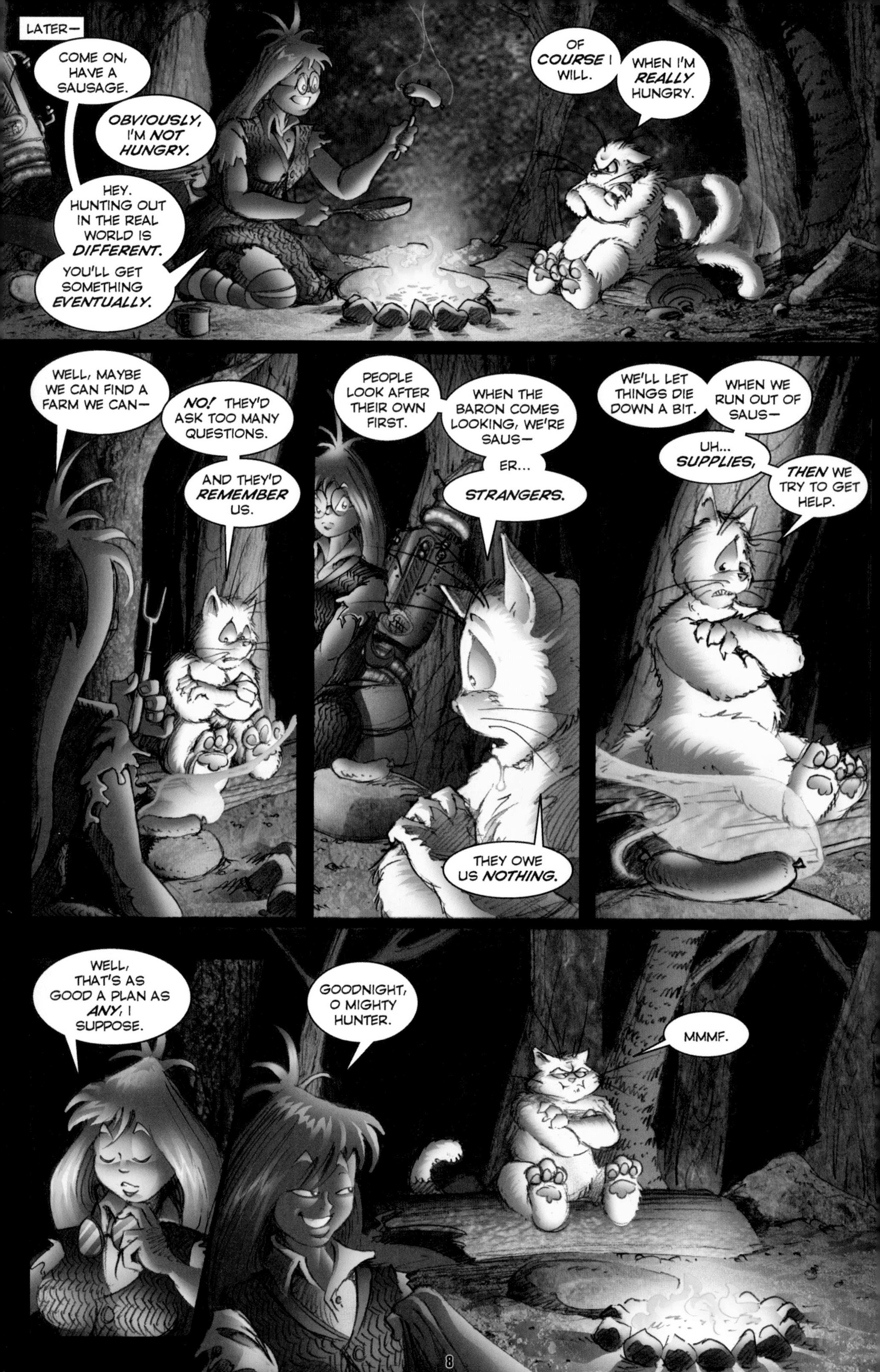
LATER—
COME ON, HAVE A SAUSAGE.
OBVIOUSLY, I'M NOT HUNGRY.
OF COURSE I WILL.
WHEN I'M REALLY HUNGRY.
HEY. HUNTING OUT IN THE REAL WORLD IS DIFFERENT.
YOU'LL GET SOMETHING EVENTUALLY.
WELL, MAYBE WE CAN FIND A FARM WE CAN—
NO! THEY'D ASK TOO MANY QUESTIONS.
AND THEY'D REMEMBER US.
PEOPLE LOOK AFTER THEIR OWN FIRST.
WHEN THE BARON COMES LOOKING, WE'RE SAUS—
ER...
STRANGERS.
THEY OWE US NOTHING.
WE'LL LET THINGS DIE DOWN A BIT.
WHEN WE RUN OUT OF SAUS—
UH... SUPPLIES,
THEN WE TRY TO GET HELP.
WELL, THAT'S AS GOOD A PLAN AS ANY, I SUPPOSE.
GOODNIGHT, O MIGHTY HUNTER.
MMMF.

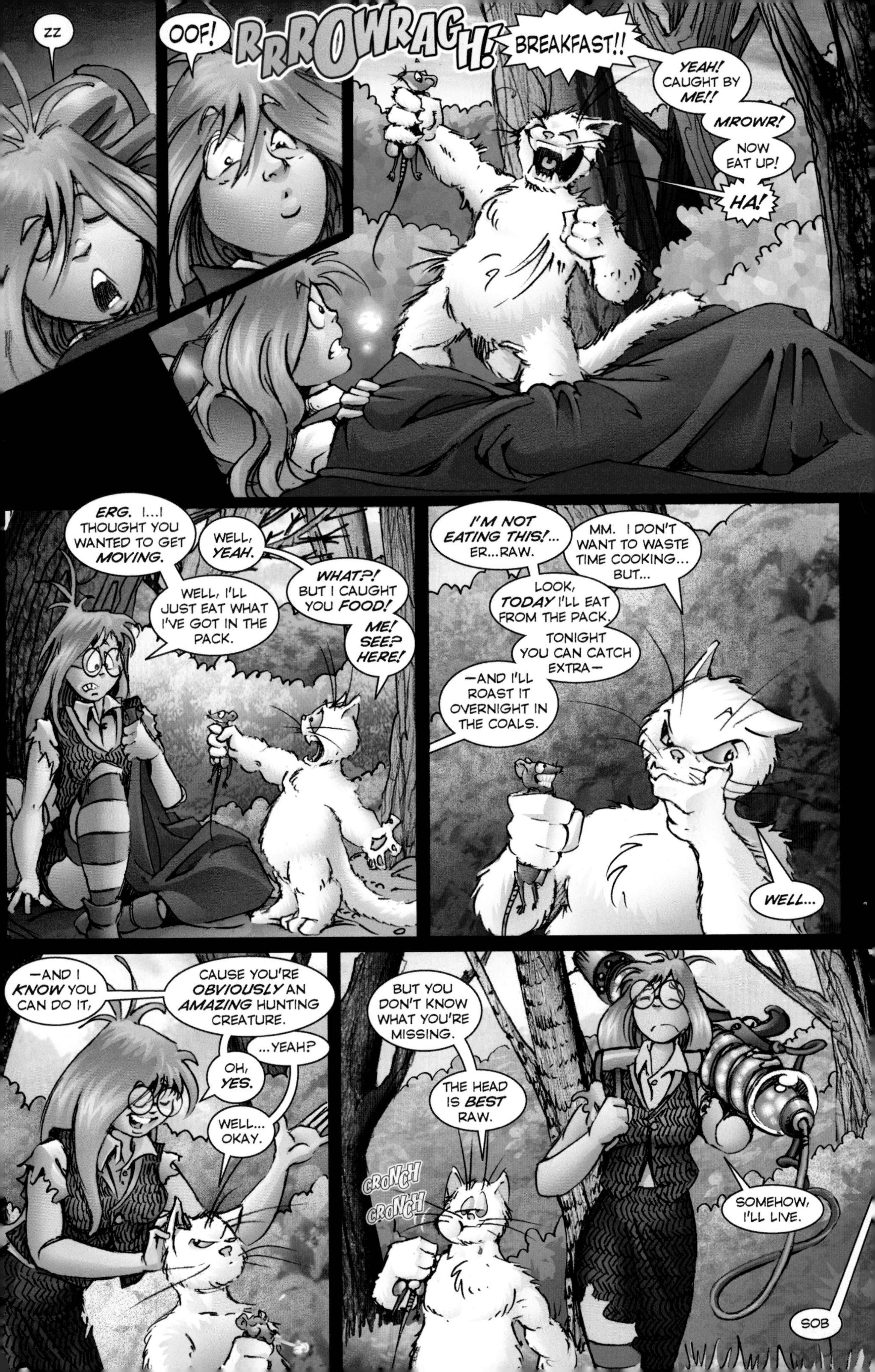
ZZ
OOF!
RRROWRAGH!
BREAKFAST!!
YEAH! CAUGHT BY ME!!
MROWR!
NOW EAT UP!
HA!
ERG. I...I THOUGHT YOU WANTED TO GET MOVING.
WELL, YEAH.
WELL, I'LL JUST EAT WHAT I'VE GOT IN THE PACK.
WHAT?! BUT I CAUGHT YOU FOOD!
ME! SEE? HERE!
I'M NOT EATING THIS!... ER...RAW.
MM. I DON'T WANT TO WASTE TIME COOKING... BUT...
LOOK, TODAY I'LL EAT FROM THE PACK.
TONIGHT YOU CAN CATCH EXTRA—
—AND I'LL ROAST IT OVERNIGHT IN THE COALS.
WELL...
—AND I KNOW YOU CAN DO IT,
CAUSE YOU'RE OBVIOUSLY AN AMAZING HUNTING CREATURE.
...YEAH?
OH, YES.
WELL... OKAY.
BUT YOU DON'T KNOW WHAT YOU'RE MISSING.
THE HEAD IS BEST RAW.
CRONCH
CRONCH
SOMEHOW, I'LL LIVE.
SOB

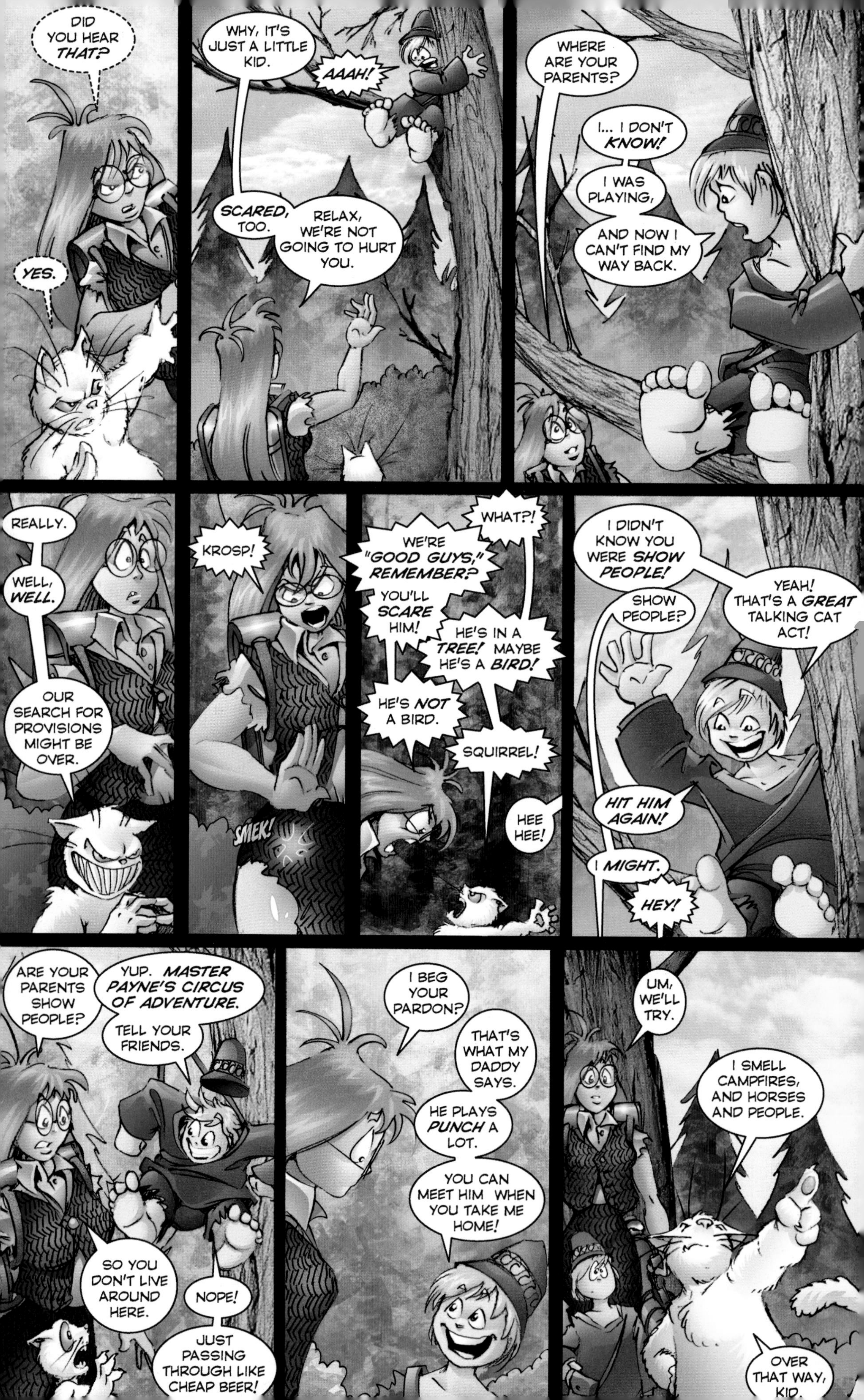
DID YOU HEAR THAT?
YES.
WHY, IT'S JUST A LITTLE KID.
AAAH!
SCARED, TOO.
RELAX, WE'RE NOT GOING TO HURT YOU.
WHERE ARE YOUR PARENTS?
I... I DON'T KNOW!
I WAS PLAYING,
AND NOW I CAN'T FIND MY WAY BACK.
REALLY.
WELL, WELL.
OUR SEARCH FOR PROVISIONS MIGHT BE OVER.
KROSP!
SMEK!
WHAT?!
WE'RE "GOOD GUYS," REMEMBER?
YOU'LL SCARE HIM!
HE'S IN A TREE! MAYBE HE'S A BIRD!
HE'S NOT A BIRD.
SQUIRREL!
HEE HEE!
I DIDN'T KNOW YOU WERE SHOW PEOPLE!
SHOW PEOPLE?
YEAH! THAT'S A GREAT TALKING CAT ACT!
HIT HIM AGAIN!
I MIGHT.
HEY!
ARE YOUR PARENTS SHOW PEOPLE?
YUP. MASTER PAYNE'S CIRCUS OF ADVENTURE.
TELL YOUR FRIENDS.
SO YOU DON'T LIVE AROUND HERE.
NOPE!
JUST PASSING THROUGH LIKE CHEAP BEER!
I BEG YOUR PARDON?
THAT'S WHAT MY DADDY SAYS.
HE PLAYS PUNCH A LOT.
YOU CAN MEET HIM WHEN YOU TAKE ME HOME!
UM, WE'LL TRY.
I SMELL CAMPFIRES, AND HORSES AND PEOPLE.
OVER THAT WAY, KID.

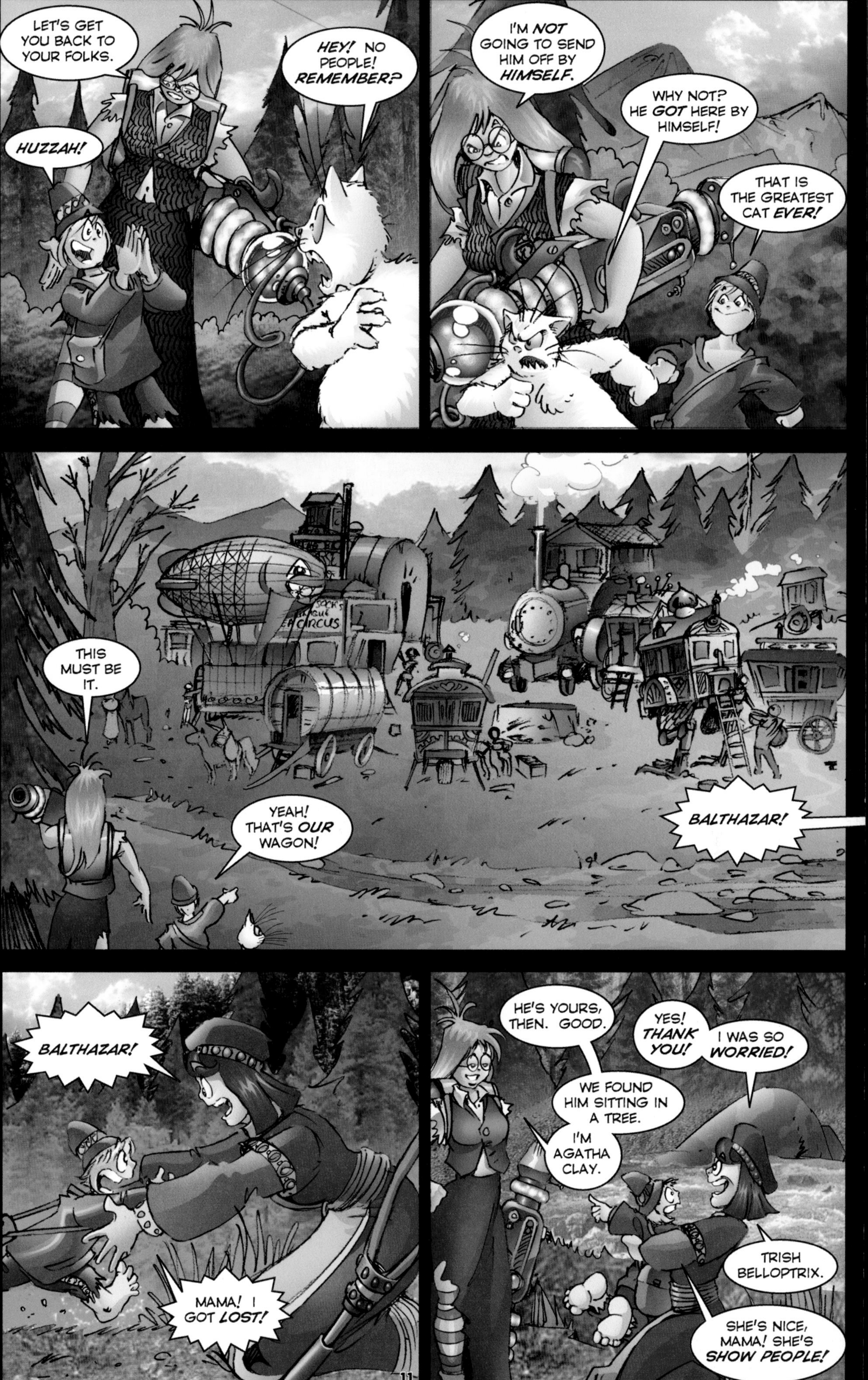
LET'S GET YOU BACK TO YOUR FOLKS.
HUZZAH!
HEY! NO PEOPLE! REMEMBER?
I'M NOT GOING TO SEND HIM OFF BY HIMSELF.
WHY NOT? HE GOT HERE BY HIMSELF!
THAT IS THE GREATEST CAT EVER!
THIS MUST BE IT.
YEAH! THAT'S OUR WAGON!
BALTHAZAR!
BALTHAZAR!
MAMA! I GOT LOST!
HE'S YOURS, THEN. GOOD.
YES! THANK YOU!
I WAS SO WORRIED!
WE FOUND HIM SITTING IN A TREE.
I'M AGATHA CLAY.
TRISH BELLOPTRIX.
SHE'S NICE, MAMA! SHE'S SHOW PEOPLE!

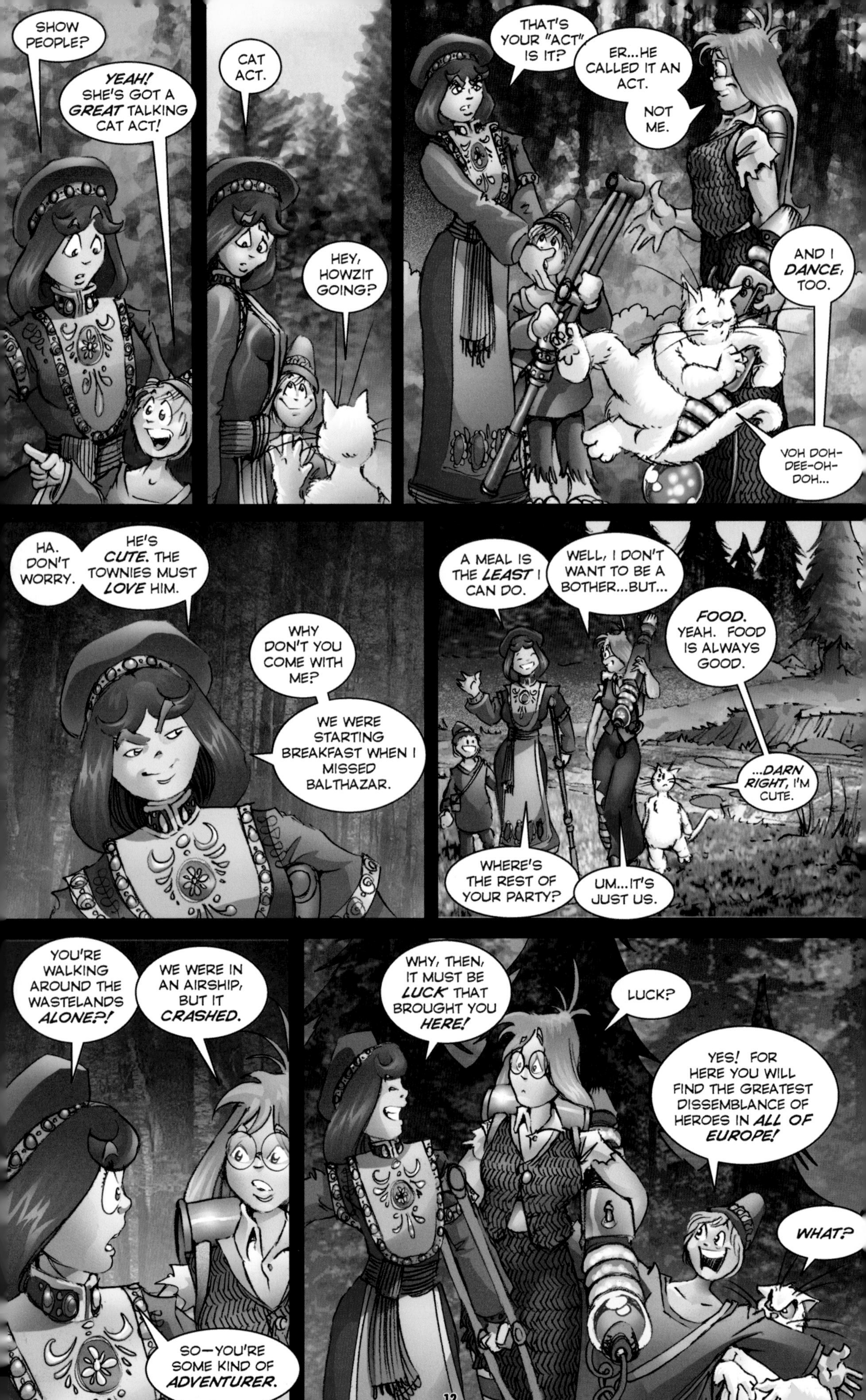

SHOW PEOPLE?
YEAH! SHE'S GOT A GREAT TALKING CAT ACT!
CAT ACT.
HEY, HOWZIT GOING?
THAT'S YOUR "ACT" IS IT?
ER...HE CALLED IT AN ACT.
NOT ME.
AND I DANCE, TOO.
VOH DOH-DEE-OH-DOH...
HA. DON'T WORRY.
HE'S CUTE. THE TOWNIES MUST LOVE HIM.
WHY DON'T YOU COME WITH ME?
WE WERE STARTING BREAKFAST WHEN I MISSED BALTHAZAR.
A MEAL IS THE LEAST I CAN DO.
WELL, I DON'T WANT TO BE A BOTHER...BUT...
FOOD. YEAH. FOOD IS ALWAYS GOOD.
...DARN RIGHT, I'M CUTE.
WHERE'S THE REST OF YOUR PARTY?
UM...IT'S JUST US.
YOU'RE WALKING AROUND THE WASTELANDS ALONE?!
WE WERE IN AN AIRSHIP, BUT IT CRASHED.
SO—YOU'RE SOME KIND OF ADVENTURER.
WHY, THEN, IT MUST BE LUCK THAT BROUGHT YOU HERE!
LUCK?
YES! FOR HERE YOU WILL FIND THE GREATEST DISSEMBLANCE OF HEROES IN ALL OF EUROPE!
WHAT?

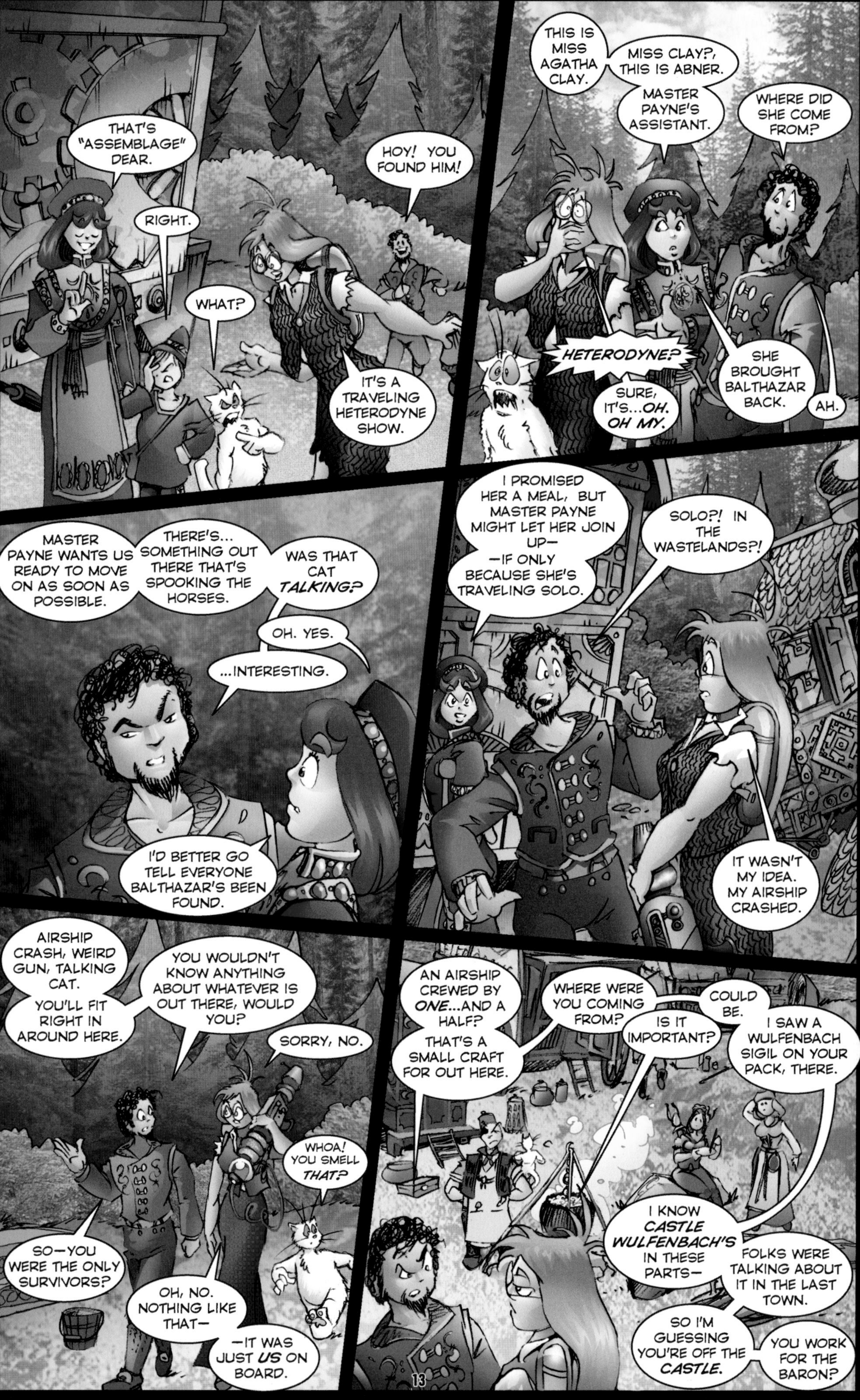
THAT'S "ASSEMBLAGE" DEAR.
RIGHT.
WHAT?
HOY! YOU FOUND HIM!
IT'S A TRAVELING HETERODYNE SHOW.
THIS IS MISS AGATHA CLAY.
MISS CLAY?, THIS IS ABNER.
MASTER PAYNE'S ASSISTANT.
WHERE DID SHE COME FROM?
HETERODYNE?
SURE, IT'S...OH. OH MY.
SHE BROUGHT BALTHAZAR BACK.
AH.
MASTER PAYNE WANTS US READY TO MOVE ON AS SOON AS POSSIBLE.
THERE'S... SOMETHING OUT THERE THAT'S SPOOKING THE HORSES.
WAS THAT CAT TALKING?
OH. YES.
...INTERESTING.
I'D BETTER GO TELL EVERYONE BALTHAZAR'S BEEN FOUND.
I PROMISED HER A MEAL, BUT MASTER PAYNE MIGHT LET HER JOIN UP—
—IF ONLY BECAUSE SHE'S TRAVELING SOLO.
SOLO?! IN THE WASTELANDS?!
IT WASN'T MY IDEA. MY AIRSHIP CRASHED.
AIRSHIP CRASH, WEIRD GUN, TALKING CAT.
YOU'LL FIT RIGHT IN AROUND HERE.
YOU WOULDN'T KNOW ANYTHING ABOUT WHATEVER IS OUT THERE, WOULD YOU?
SORRY, NO.
WHOA! YOU SMELL THAT?
SO—YOU WERE THE ONLY SURVIVORS?
OH, NO. NOTHING LIKE THAT—
—IT WAS JUST US ON BOARD.
AN AIRSHIP CREWED BY ONE...AND A HALF?
THAT'S A SMALL CRAFT FOR OUT HERE.
WHERE WERE YOU COMING FROM?
IS IT IMPORTANT?
COULD BE.
I SAW A WULFENBACH SIGIL ON YOUR PACK, THERE.
I KNOW CASTLE WULFENBACH'S IN THESE PARTS—
FOLKS WERE TALKING ABOUT IT IN THE LAST TOWN.
SO I'M GUESSING YOU'RE OFF THE CASTLE.
YOU WORK FOR THE BARON?

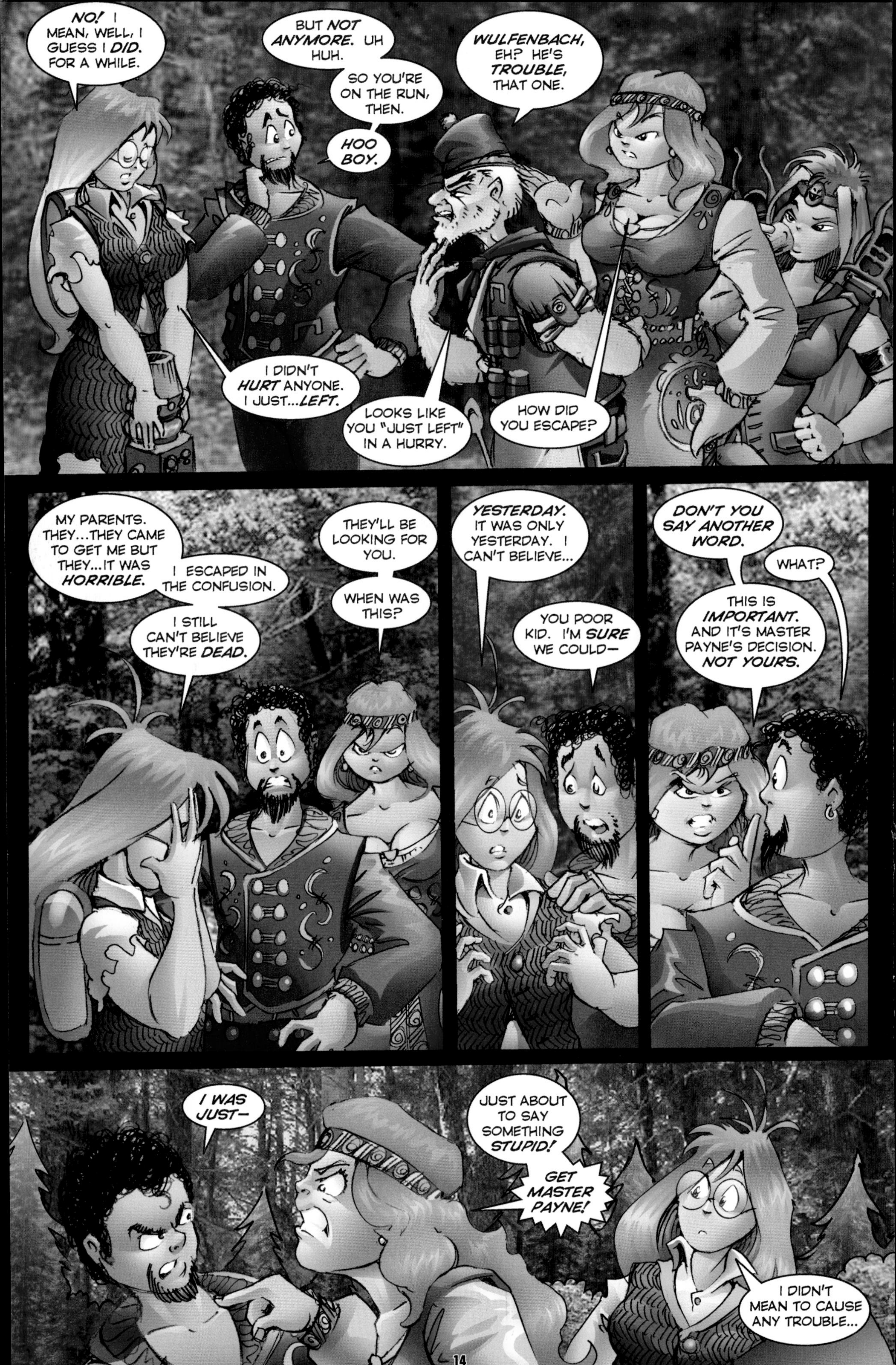
NO! I MEAN, WELL, I GUESS I DID. FOR A WHILE.
BUT NOT ANYMORE. UH HUH.
SO YOU'RE ON THE RUN, THEN.
HOO BOY.
WULFENBACH, EH? HE'S TROUBLE, THAT ONE.
I DIDN'T HURT ANYONE. I JUST...LEFT.
LOOKS LIKE YOU "JUST LEFT" IN A HURRY.
HOW DID YOU ESCAPE?
MY PARENTS. THEY...THEY CAME TO GET ME BUT THEY...IT WAS HORRIBLE.
I ESCAPED IN THE CONFUSION.
I STILL CAN'T BELIEVE THEY'RE DEAD.
THEY'LL BE LOOKING FOR YOU.
WHEN WAS THIS?
YESTERDAY. IT WAS ONLY YESTERDAY. I CAN'T BELIEVE...
YOU POOR KID. I'M SURE WE COULD—
DON'T YOU SAY ANOTHER WORD.
WHAT?
THIS IS IMPORTANT. AND IT'S MASTER PAYNE'S DECISION. NOT YOURS.
I WAS JUST—
JUST ABOUT TO SAY SOMETHING STUPID!
GET MASTER PAYNE!
I DIDN'T MEAN TO CAUSE ANY TROUBLE...

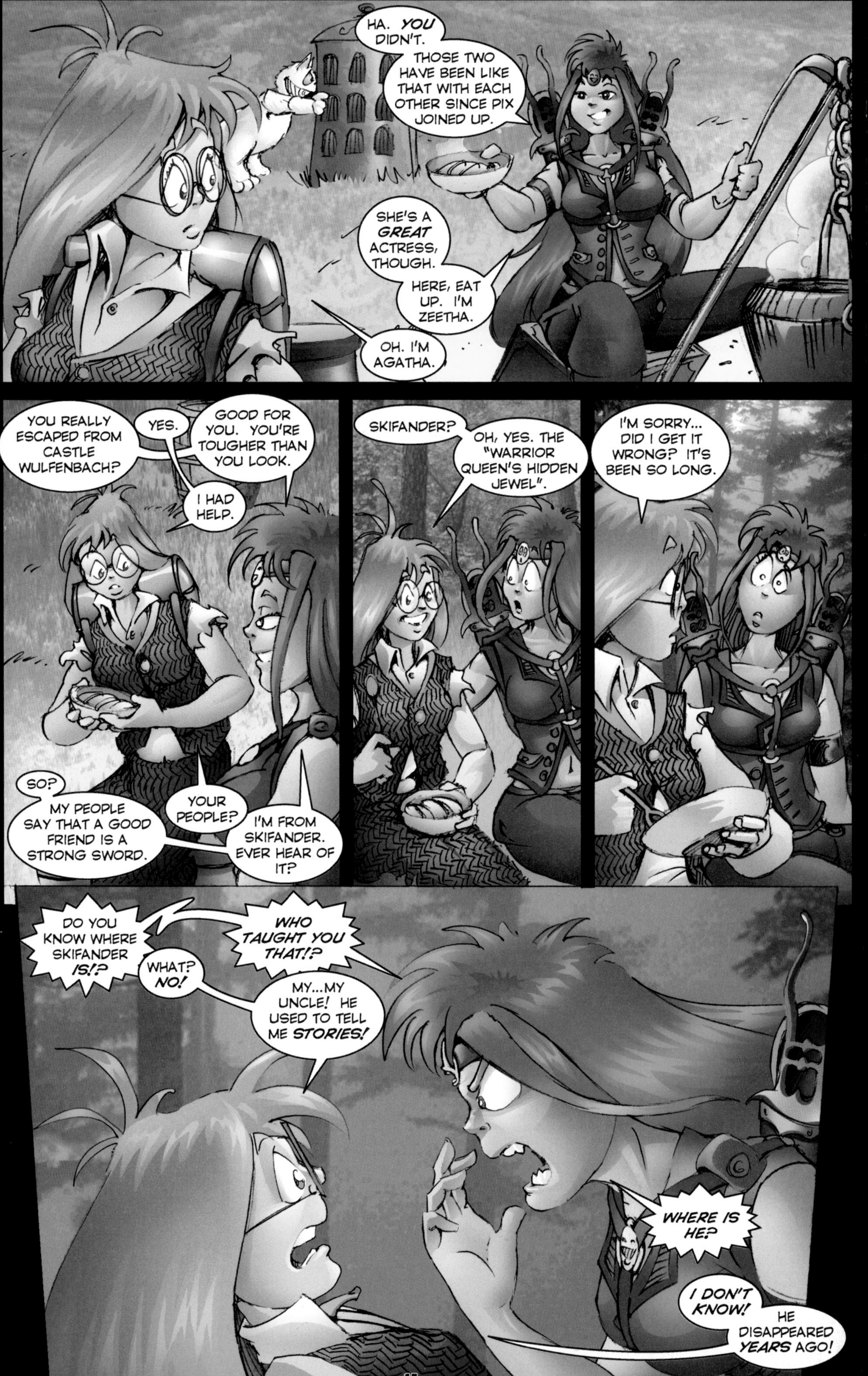

HA. *YOU* DIDN'T.
THOSE TWO HAVE BEEN LIKE THAT WITH EACH OTHER SINCE PIX JOINED UP.
SHE'S A *GREAT* ACTRESS, THOUGH.
HERE, EAT UP. I'M ZEETHA.
OH. I'M AGATHA.
YOU REALLY ESCAPED FROM CASTLE WULFENBACH?
YES.
GOOD FOR YOU. YOU'RE TOUGHER THAN YOU LOOK.
I HAD HELP.
SO?
MY PEOPLE SAY THAT A GOOD FRIEND IS A STRONG SWORD.
YOUR PEOPLE?
I'M FROM SKIFANDER. EVER HEAR OF IT?
SKIFANDER?
OH, YES. THE "WARRIOR QUEEN'S HIDDEN JEWEL".
I'M SORRY... DID I GET IT WRONG? IT'S BEEN SO LONG.
WHO TAUGHT YOU THAT!?
MY...MY UNCLE! HE USED TO TELL ME *STORIES!*
DO YOU KNOW WHERE SKIFANDER *IS!?*
WHAT? *NO!*
WHERE IS HE?
I DON'T KNOW!
HE DISAPPEARED *YEARS* AGO!

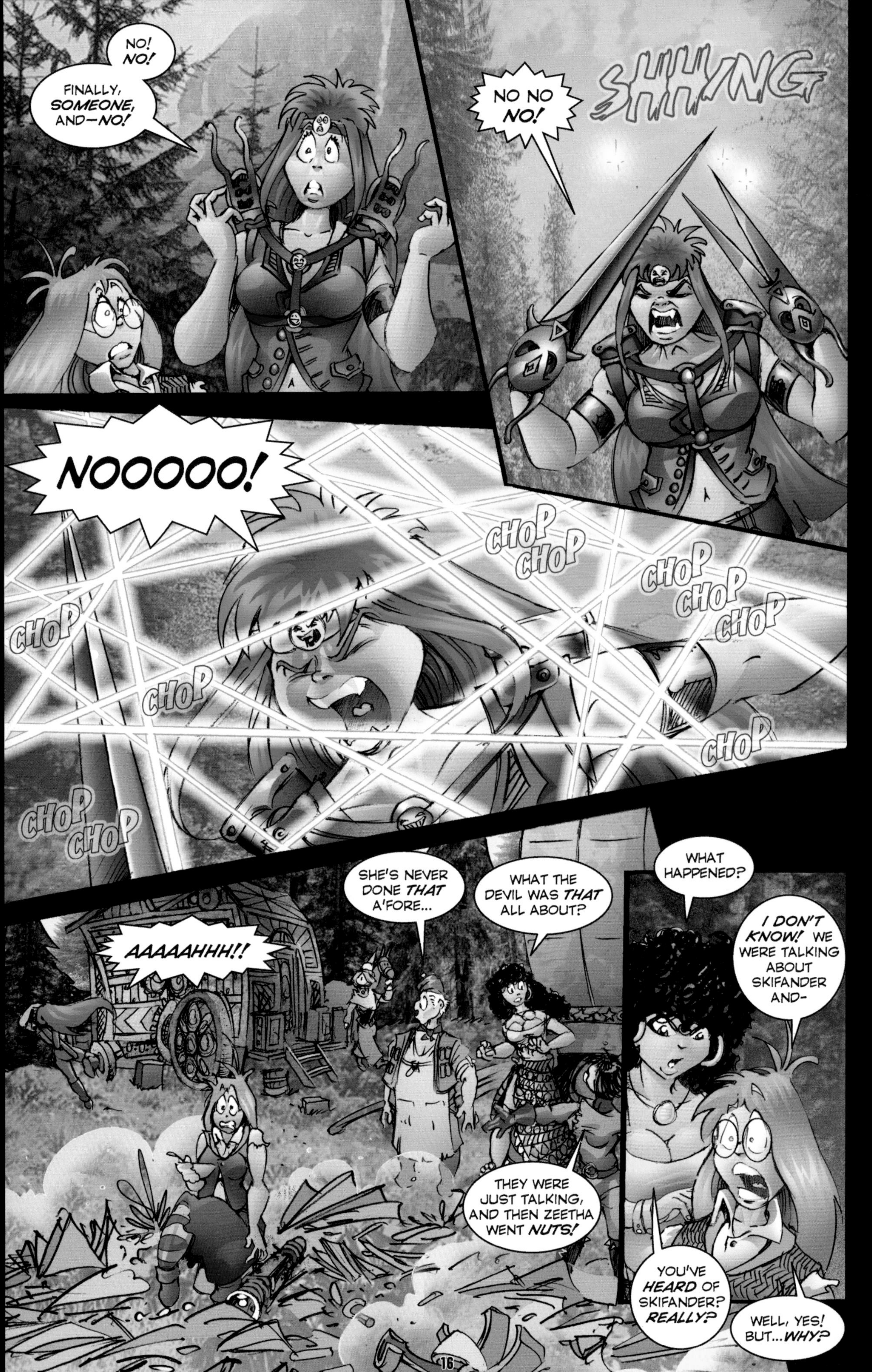
NO! NO!
FINALLY, SOMEONE, AND—NO!
NO NO NO!
SHHYNG
NOOOOO!
CHOP CHOP
CHOP CHOP CHOP
CHOP
CHOP
CHOP
CHOP CHOP
AAAAAHHH!!
SHE'S NEVER DONE THAT A'FORE...
WHAT THE DEVIL WAS THAT ALL ABOUT?
THEY WERE JUST TALKING, AND THEN ZEETHA WENT NUTS!
WHAT HAPPENED?
I DON'T KNOW! WE WERE TALKING ABOUT SKIFANDER AND-
YOU'VE HEARD OF SKIFANDER? REALLY?
WELL, YES! BUT...WHY?

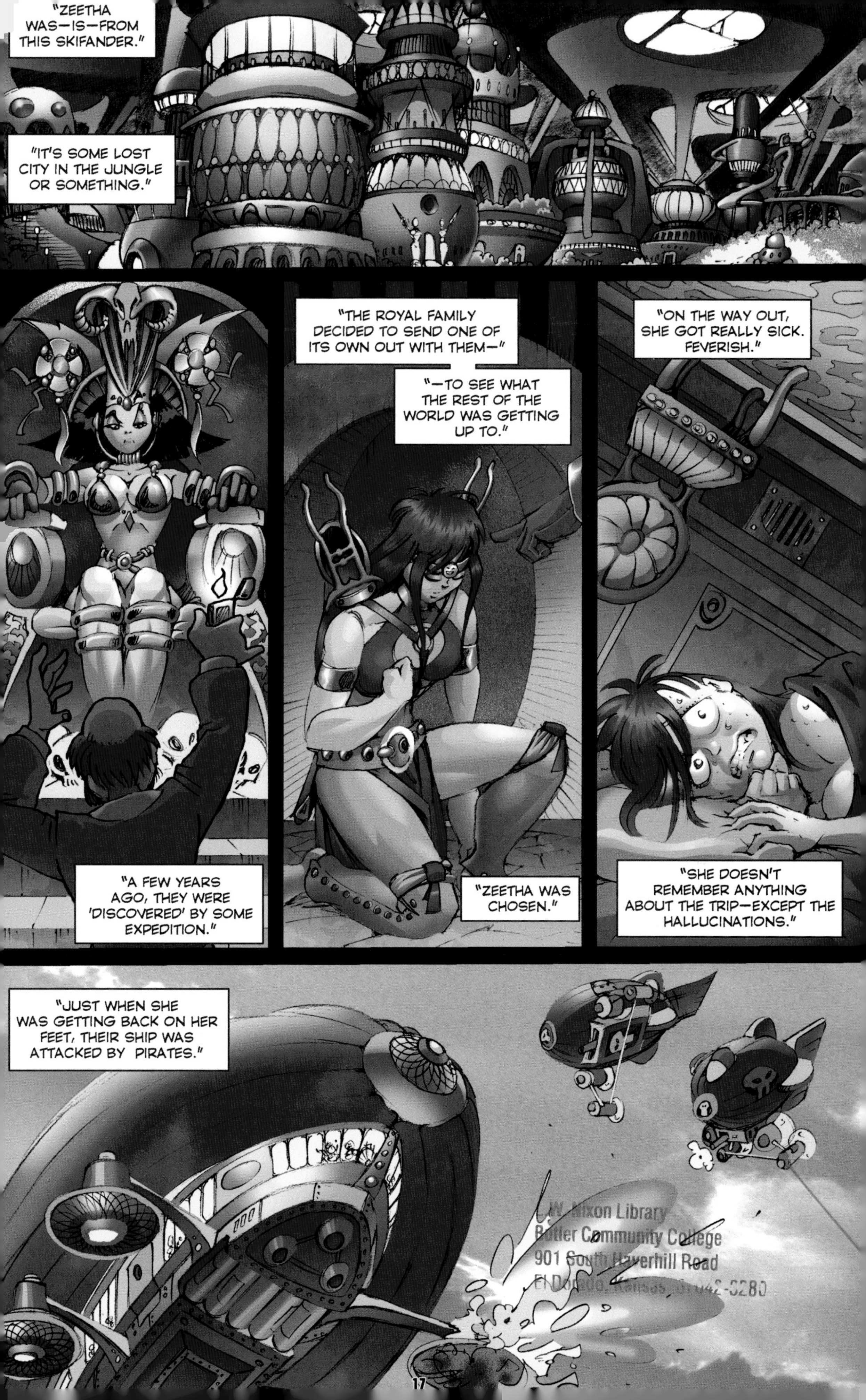
"ZEETHA WAS—IS—FROM THIS SKIFANDER."
"IT'S SOME LOST CITY IN THE JUNGLE OR SOMETHING."
"A FEW YEARS AGO, THEY WERE 'DISCOVERED' BY SOME EXPEDITION."
"THE ROYAL FAMILY DECIDED TO SEND ONE OF ITS OWN OUT WITH THEM—"
"—TO SEE WHAT THE REST OF THE WORLD WAS GETTING UP TO."
"ZEETHA WAS CHOSEN."
"ON THE WAY OUT, SHE GOT REALLY SICK. FEVERISH."
"SHE DOESN'T REMEMBER ANYTHING ABOUT THE TRIP—EXCEPT THE HALLUCINATIONS."
"JUST WHEN SHE WAS GETTING BACK ON HER FEET, THEIR SHIP WAS ATTACKED BY PIRATES."

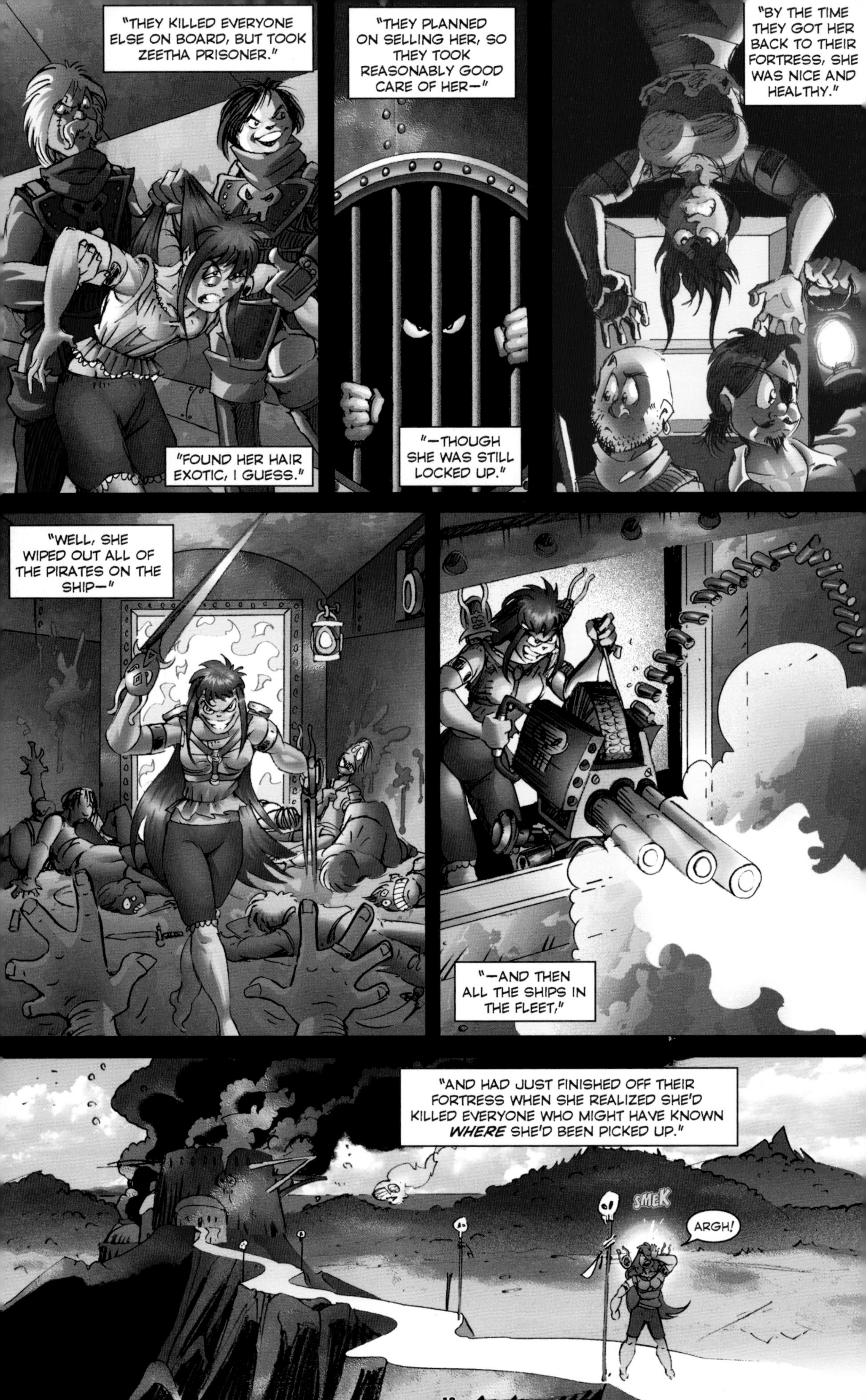
"THEY KILLED EVERYONE ELSE ON BOARD, BUT TOOK ZEETHA PRISONER."
"FOUND HER HAIR EXOTIC, I GUESS."
"THEY PLANNED ON SELLING HER, SO THEY TOOK REASONABLY GOOD CARE OF HER—"
"—THOUGH SHE WAS STILL LOCKED UP."
"BY THE TIME THEY GOT HER BACK TO THEIR FORTRESS, SHE WAS NICE AND HEALTHY."
"WELL, SHE WIPED OUT ALL OF THE PIRATES ON THE SHIP—"
"—AND THEN ALL THE SHIPS IN THE FLEET,"
"AND HAD JUST FINISHED OFF THEIR FORTRESS WHEN SHE REALIZED SHE'D KILLED EVERYONE WHO MIGHT HAVE KNOWN *WHERE* SHE'D BEEN PICKED UP."
SMEK
ARGH!

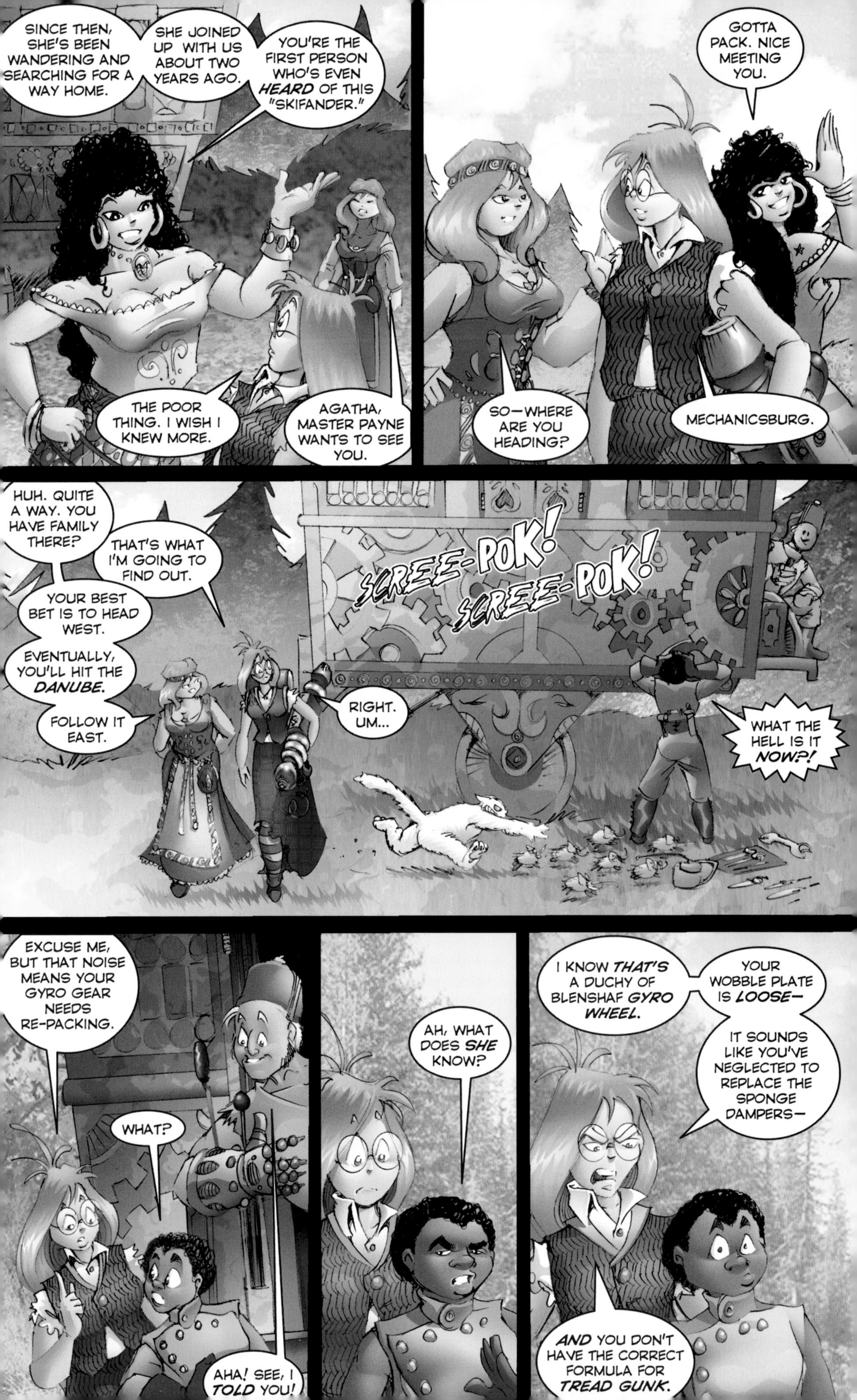
SINCE THEN, SHE'S BEEN WANDERING AND SEARCHING FOR A WAY HOME.
SHE JOINED UP WITH US ABOUT TWO YEARS AGO.
YOU'RE THE FIRST PERSON WHO'S EVEN *HEARD* OF THIS "SKIFANDER."
THE POOR THING. I WISH I KNEW MORE.
AGATHA, MASTER PAYNE WANTS TO SEE YOU.
GOTTA PACK. NICE MEETING YOU.
SO—WHERE ARE YOU HEADING?
MECHANICSBURG.
HUH. QUITE A WAY. YOU HAVE FAMILY THERE?
THAT'S WHAT I'M GOING TO FIND OUT.
YOUR BEST BET IS TO HEAD WEST.
EVENTUALLY, YOU'LL HIT THE *DANUBE.*
FOLLOW IT EAST.
SCREE-POK! SCREE-POK!
RIGHT. UM...
WHAT THE HELL IS IT *NOW?!*
EXCUSE ME, BUT THAT NOISE MEANS YOUR GYRO GEAR NEEDS RE-PACKING.
WHAT?
AHA! SEE, I *TOLD* YOU!
AH, WHAT DOES *SHE* KNOW?
I KNOW *THAT'S* A DUCHY OF BLENSHAF *GYRO WHEEL.*
YOUR WOBBLE PLATE IS *LOOSE—*
IT SOUNDS LIKE YOU'VE NEGLECTED TO REPLACE THE SPONGE DAMPERS—
AND YOU DON'T HAVE THE CORRECT FORMULA FOR *TREAD GUNK.*

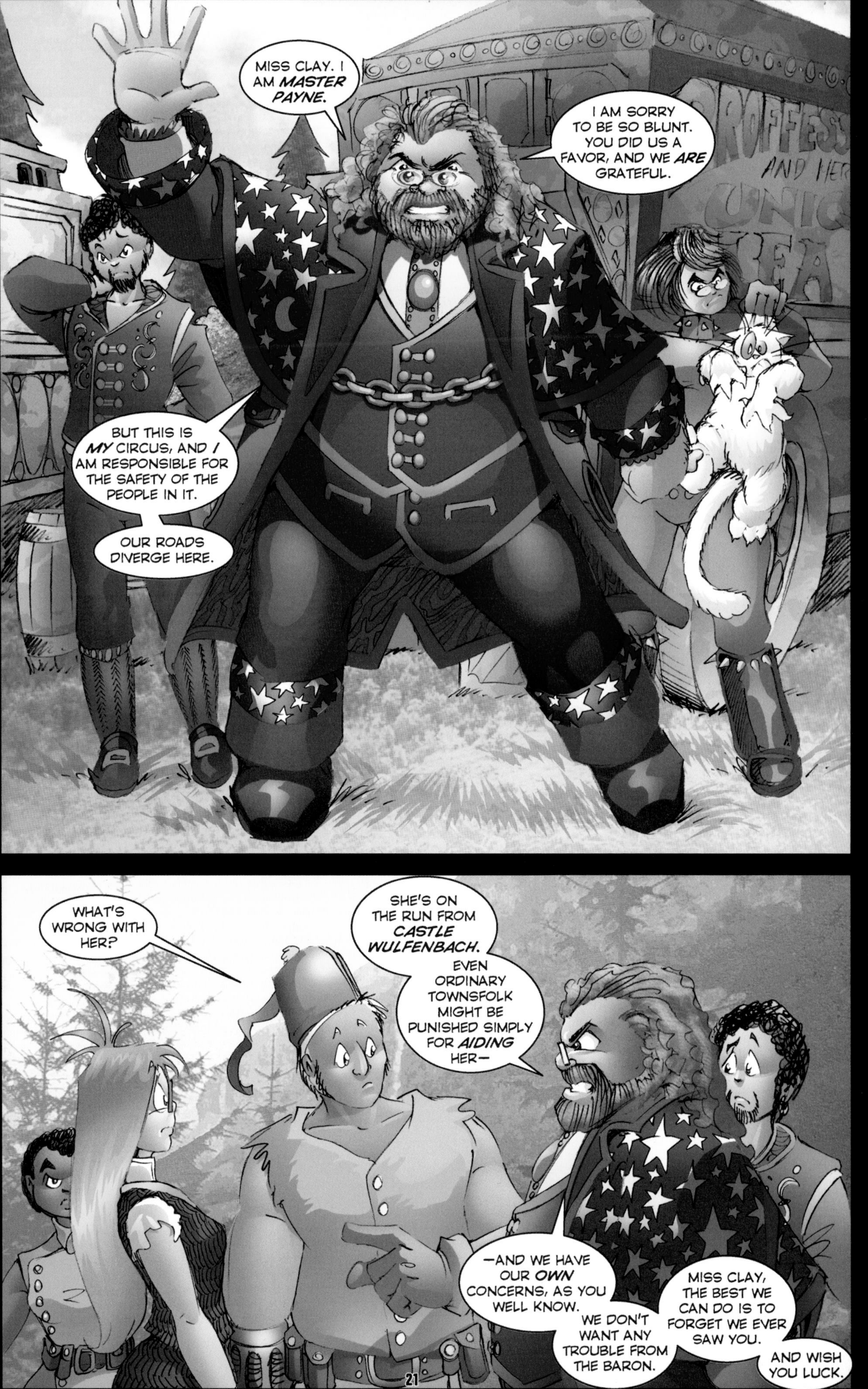
MISS CLAY. I AM *MASTER PAYNE.*
I AM SORRY TO BE SO BLUNT. YOU DID US A FAVOR, AND WE *ARE* GRATEFUL.
BUT THIS IS *MY* CIRCUS, AND *I* AM RESPONSIBLE FOR THE SAFETY OF THE PEOPLE IN IT.
OUR ROADS DIVERGE HERE.
WHAT'S WRONG WITH HER?
SHE'S ON THE RUN FROM *CASTLE WULFENBACH.*
EVEN ORDINARY TOWNSFOLK MIGHT BE PUNISHED SIMPLY FOR *AIDING* HER—
—AND WE HAVE OUR *OWN* CONCERNS, AS YOU WELL KNOW.
WE DON'T WANT ANY TROUBLE FROM THE BARON.
MISS CLAY, THE BEST WE CAN DO IS TO FORGET WE EVER SAW YOU.
AND WISH YOU LUCK.

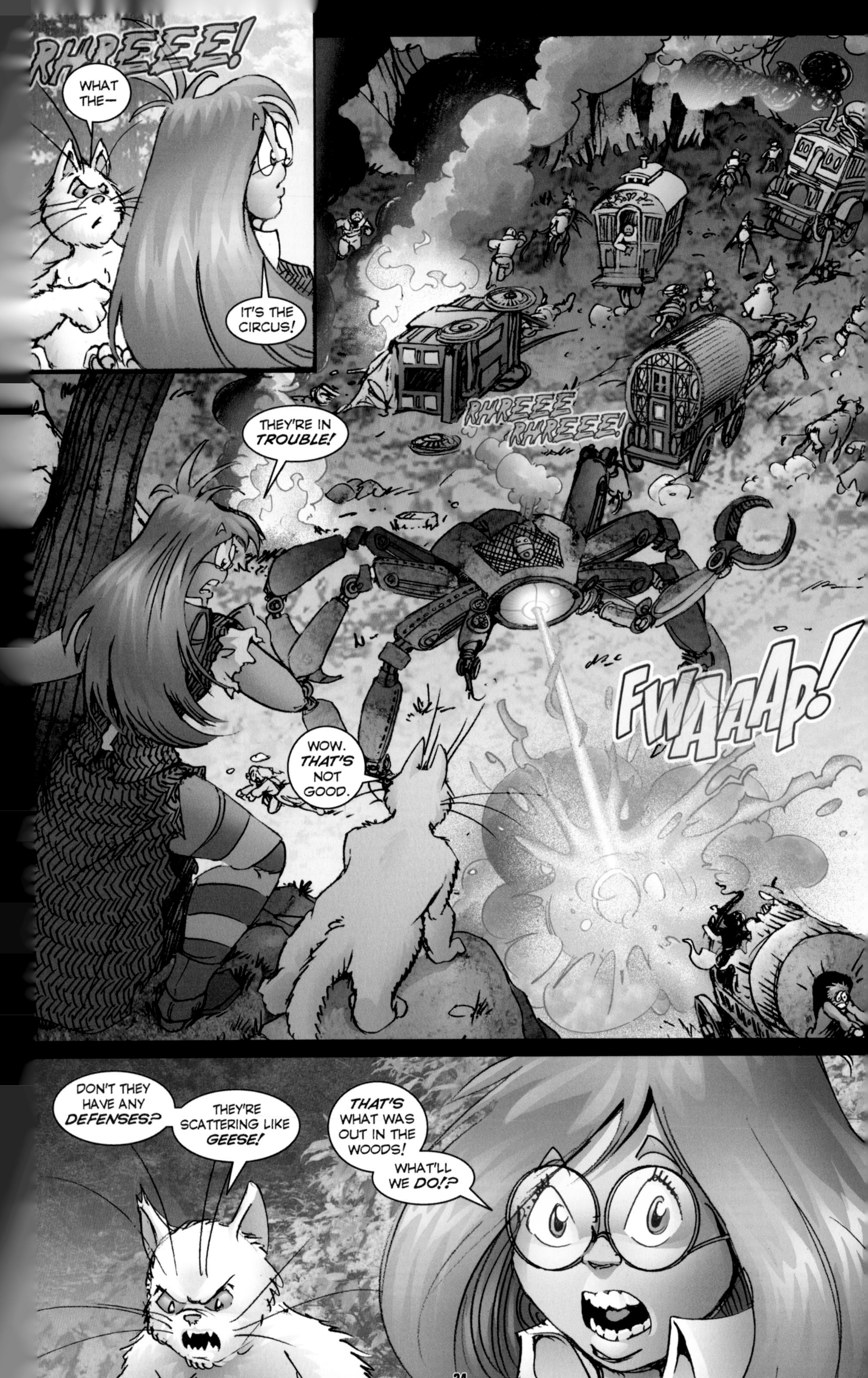
RHREEE!
WHAT THE—
IT'S THE CIRCUS!
RHREEE RHREEE!
THEY'RE IN TROUBLE!
WOW. THAT'S NOT GOOD.
FWAAAP!
DON'T THEY HAVE ANY DEFENSES?
THEY'RE SCATTERING LIKE GEESE!
THAT'S WHAT WAS OUT IN THE WOODS!
WHAT'LL WE DO!?

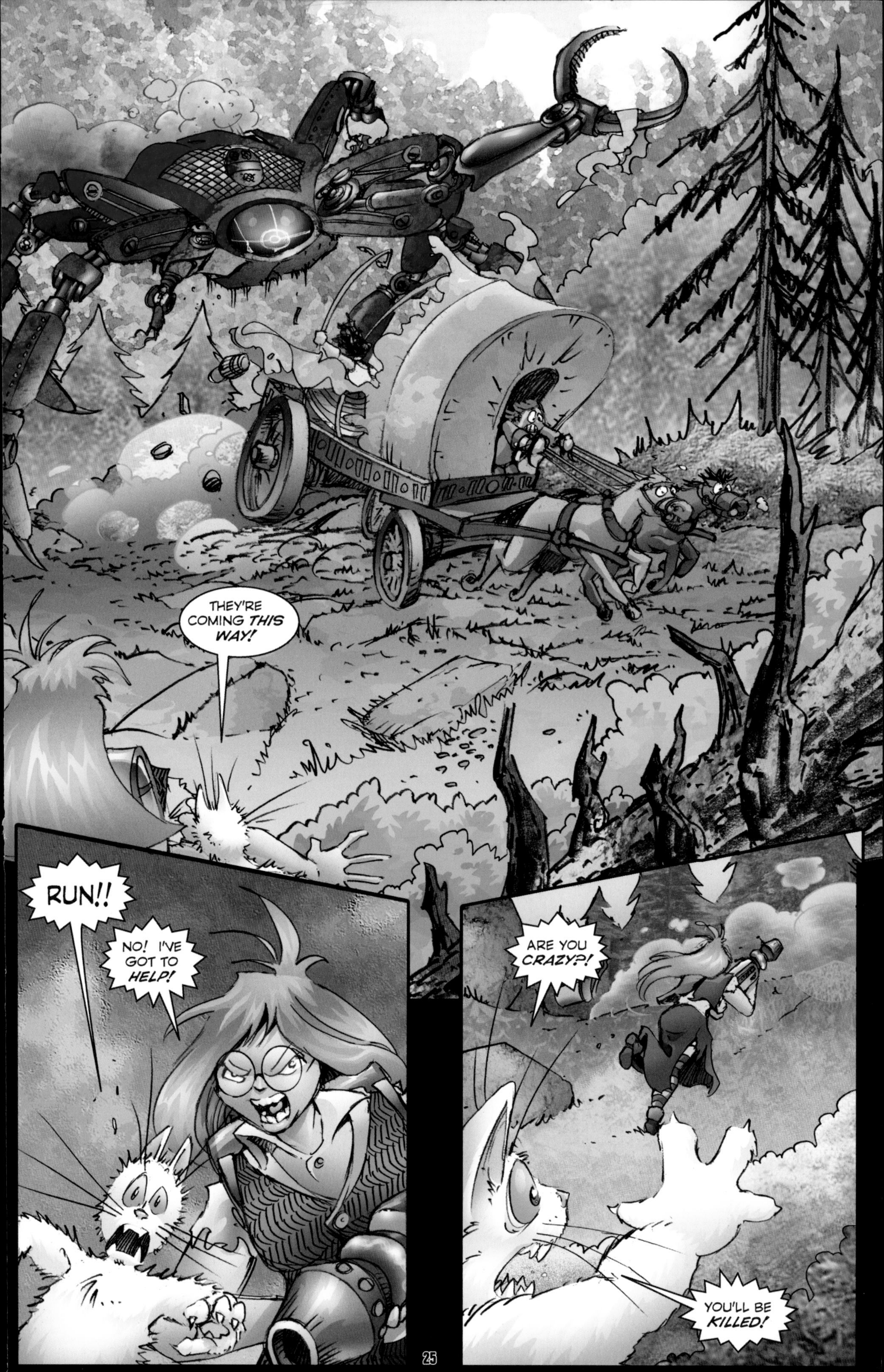
THEY'RE COMING THIS WAY!
RUN!!
NO! I'VE GOT TO HELP!
ARE YOU CRAZY?!
YOU'LL BE KILLED!

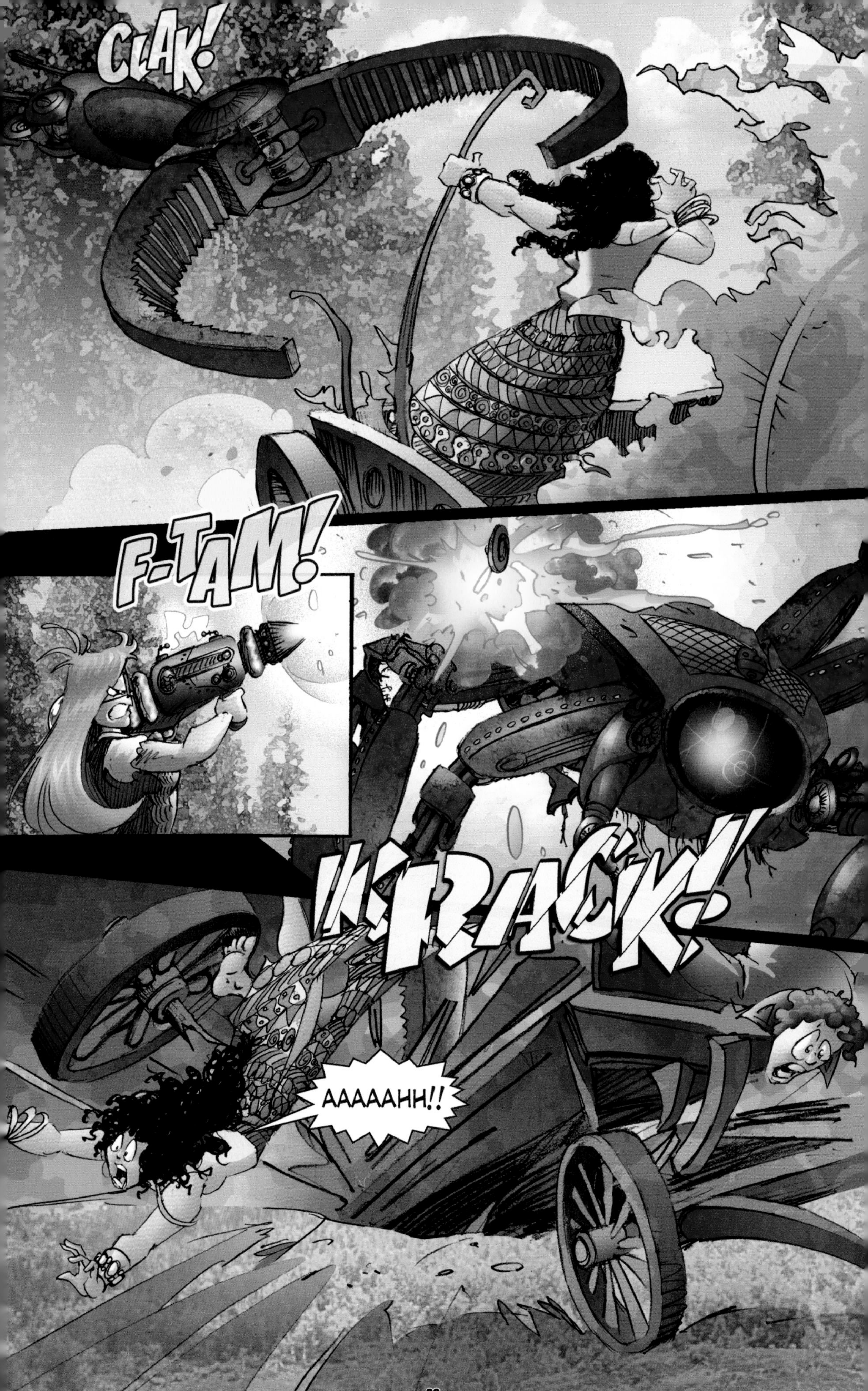
CLAK!
F-TAM!
KRACK!
AAAAAHH!!

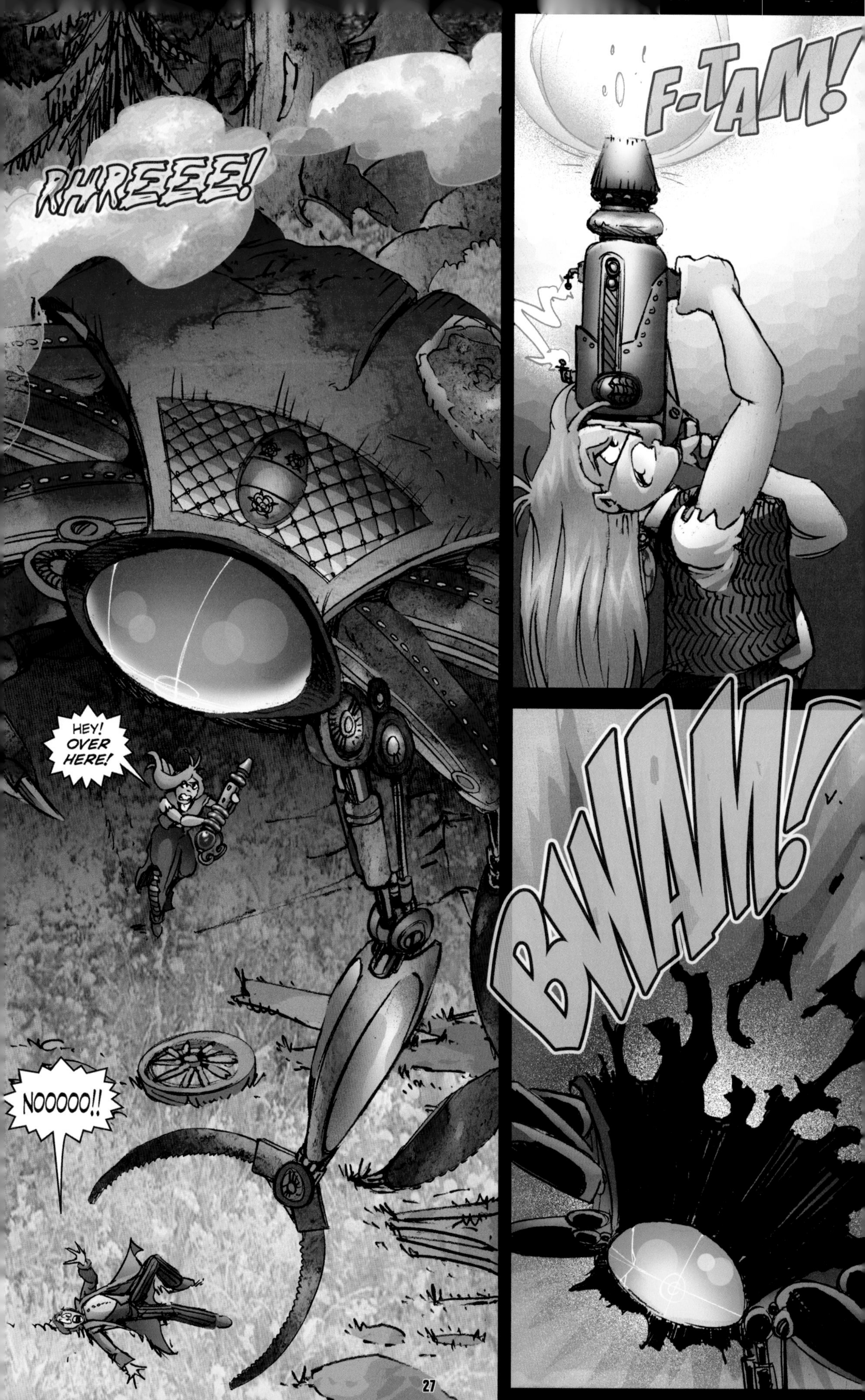

RHREEE!
HEY! OVER HERE!
NOOOOO!!
F-TAM!
BWAM!

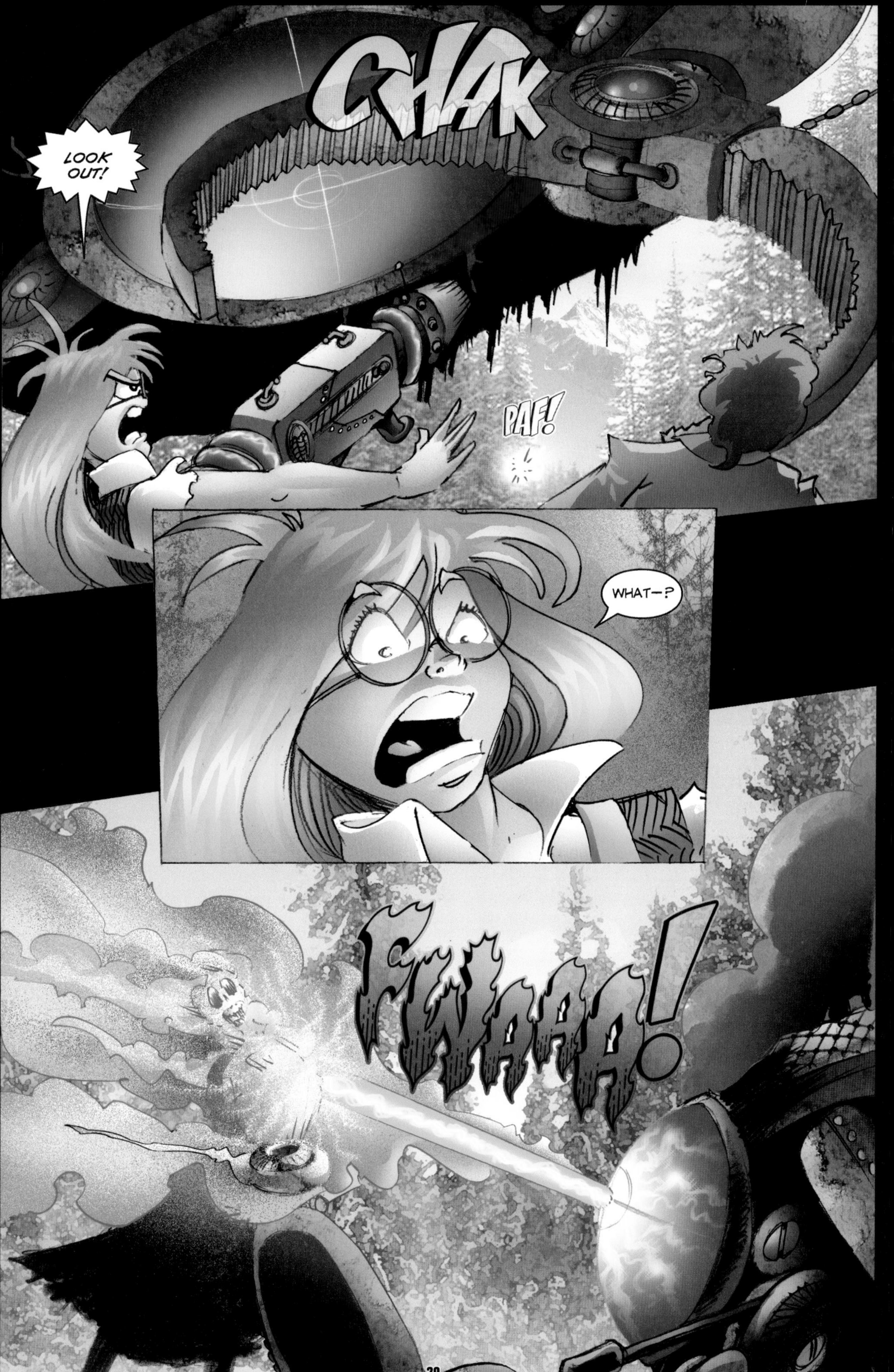
CHAK
LOOK OUT!
PAF!
WHAT–?
FWAAA!

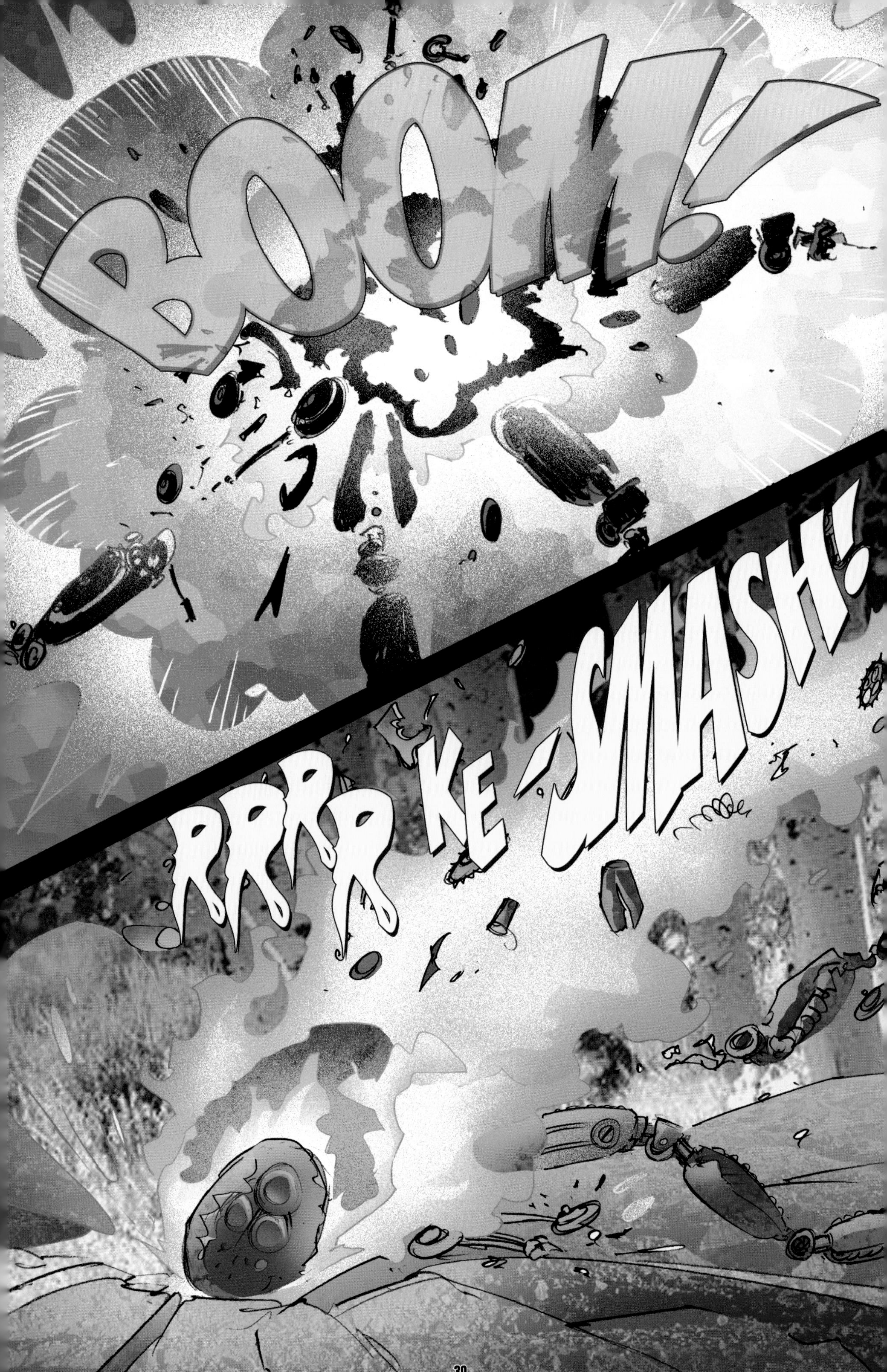
BOOM!
RRRR KE-SMASH!

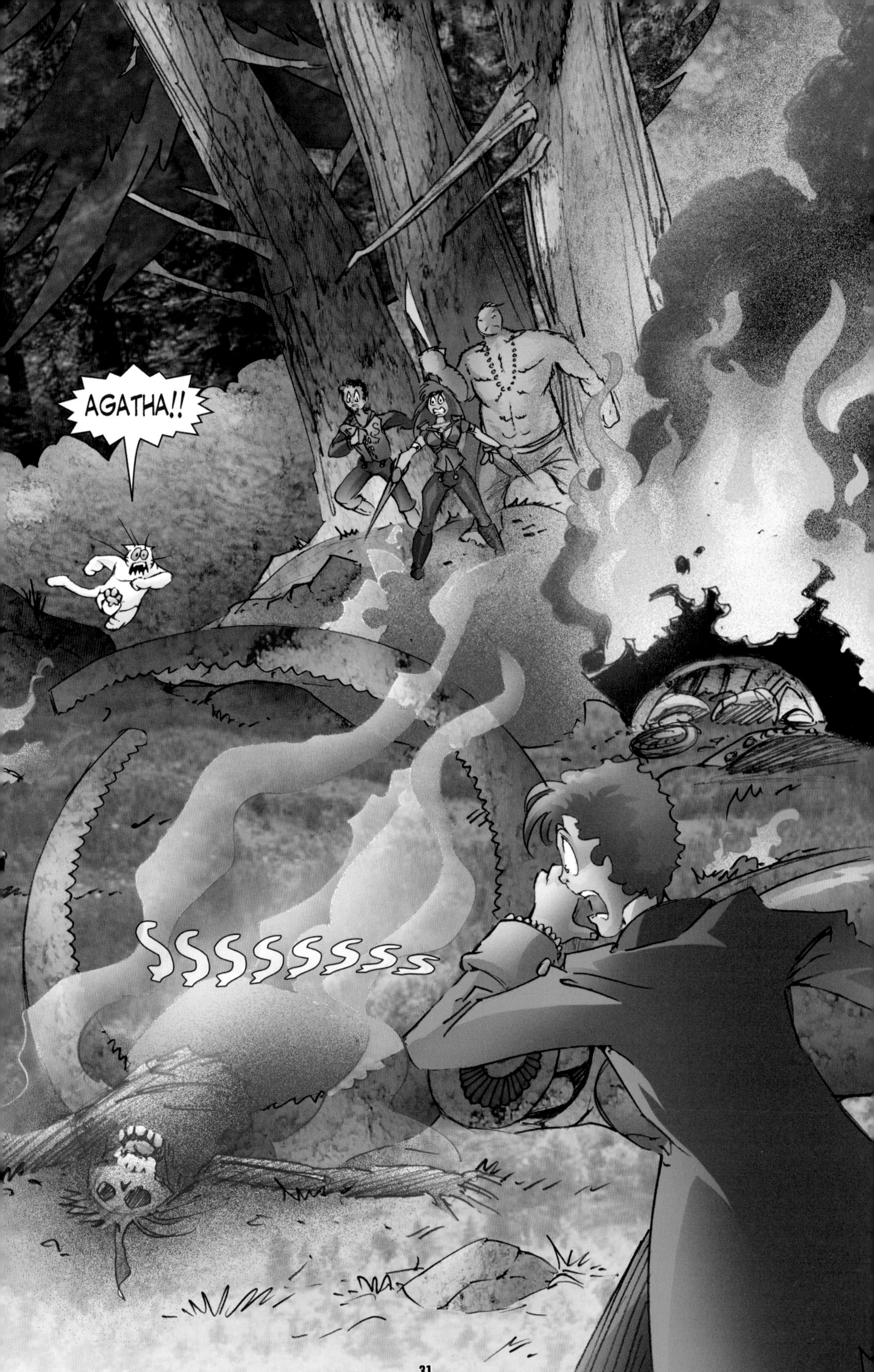
AGATHA!!
SSSSSSSSS

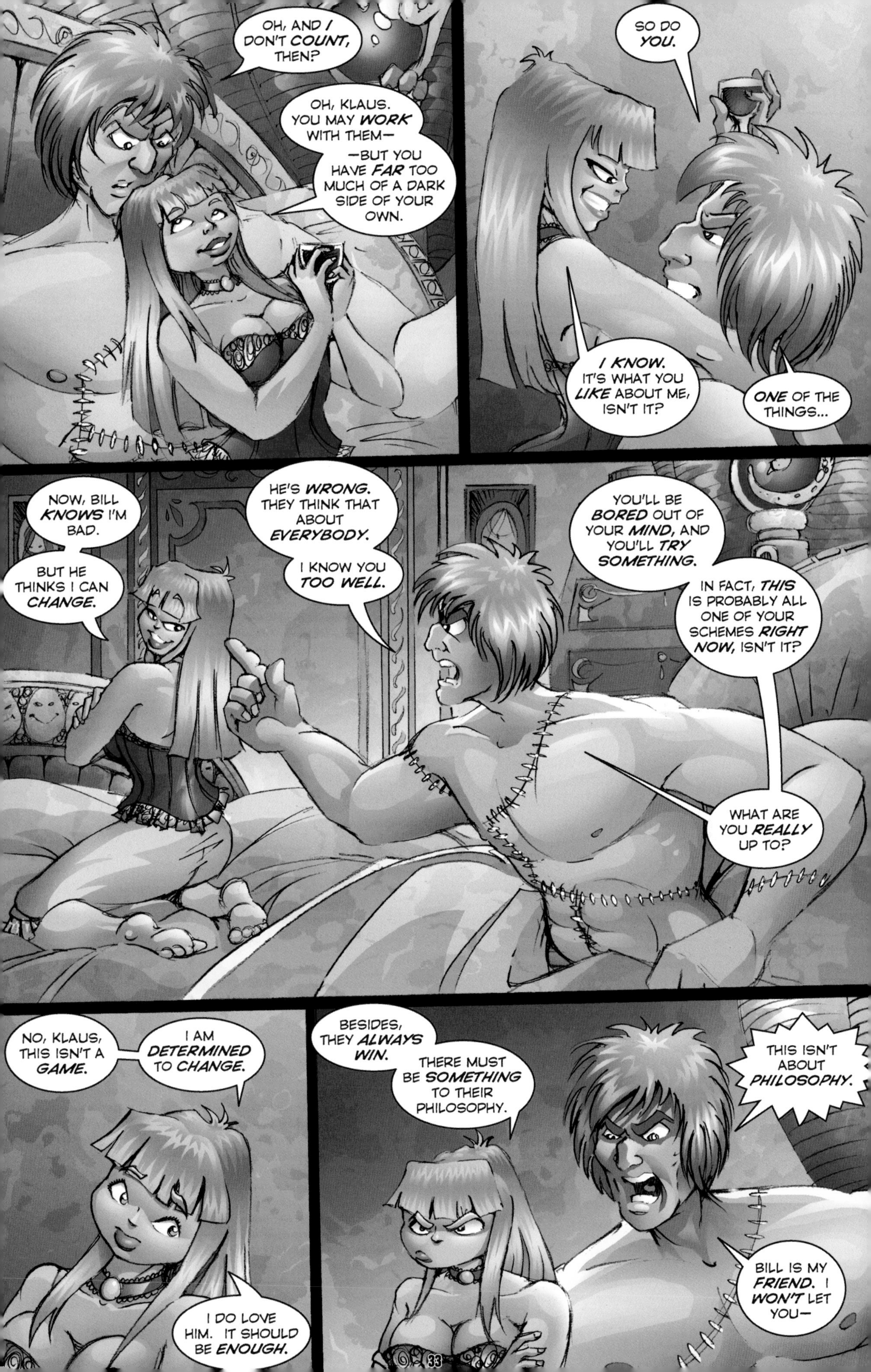
OH, AND I DON'T COUNT, THEN?
OH, KLAUS. YOU MAY WORK WITH THEM—
—BUT YOU HAVE FAR TOO MUCH OF A DARK SIDE OF YOUR OWN.
SO DO YOU.
I KNOW. IT'S WHAT YOU LIKE ABOUT ME, ISN'T IT?
ONE OF THE THINGS...
NOW, BILL KNOWS I'M BAD.
BUT HE THINKS I CAN CHANGE.
HE'S WRONG. THEY THINK THAT ABOUT EVERYBODY.
I KNOW YOU TOO WELL.
YOU'LL BE BORED OUT OF YOUR MIND, AND YOU'LL TRY SOMETHING.
IN FACT, THIS IS PROBABLY ALL ONE OF YOUR SCHEMES RIGHT NOW, ISN'T IT?
WHAT ARE YOU REALLY UP TO?
NO, KLAUS, THIS ISN'T A GAME.
I AM DETERMINED TO CHANGE.
I DO LOVE HIM. IT SHOULD BE ENOUGH.
BESIDES, THEY ALWAYS WIN.
THERE MUST BE SOMETHING TO THEIR PHILOSOPHY.
THIS ISN'T ABOUT PHILOSOPHY.
BILL IS MY FRIEND. I WON'T LET YOU—

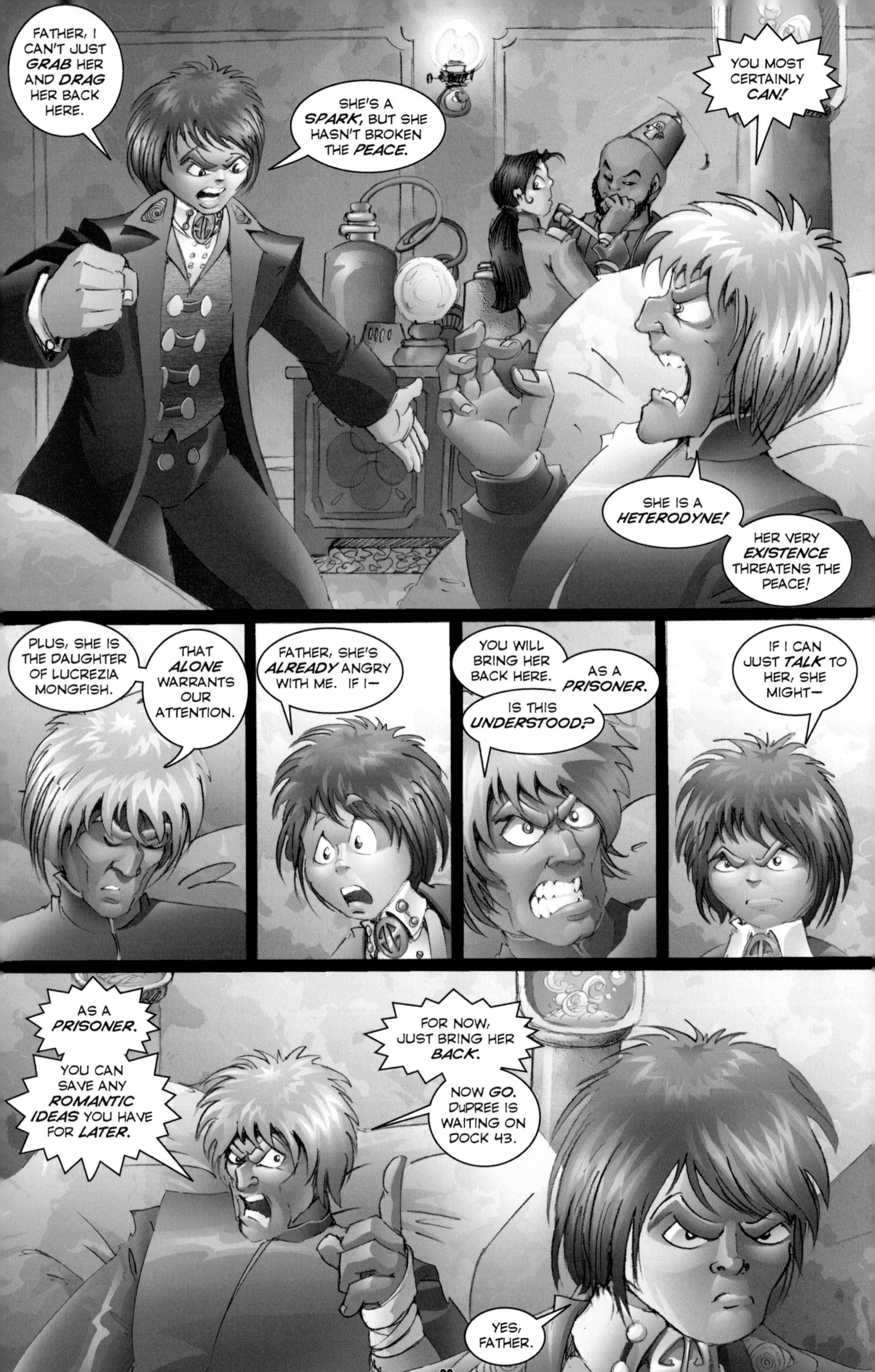

FATHER, I CAN'T JUST GRAB HER AND DRAG HER BACK HERE.
SHE'S A SPARK, BUT SHE HASN'T BROKEN THE PEACE.
YOU MOST CERTAINLY CAN!
SHE IS A HETERODYNE!
HER VERY EXISTENCE THREATENS THE PEACE!
PLUS, SHE IS THE DAUGHTER OF LUCREZIA MONGFISH.
THAT ALONE WARRANTS OUR ATTENTION.
FATHER, SHE'S ALREADY ANGRY WITH ME. IF I—
YOU WILL BRING HER BACK HERE.
AS A PRISONER.
IS THIS UNDERSTOOD?
IF I CAN JUST TALK TO HER, SHE MIGHT—
AS A PRISONER.
YOU CAN SAVE ANY ROMANTIC IDEAS YOU HAVE FOR LATER.
FOR NOW, JUST BRING HER BACK.
NOW GO. DuPREE IS WAITING ON DOCK 43.
YES, FATHER.

39

NOT BE *HARMED*?!

HOW AM I SUPPOSED TO *WORK* HERE?

THESE PEOPLE MAY KNOW *NOTHING*.

OH, *DON'T* START *THAT* AGAIN.

I FOUND THE CRASH SITE—

—THE PLACE SHE SLEPT—

—AND TRACKS OF A CARAVAN GOING *RIGHT PAST* ON THE *SAME DAY*.

I *KNOW* YOU'RE *GOOD*,

BUT *THIS TIME* WE WANT THE JOB DONE *WITHOUT INCIDENT*.

IT'S NOT *MY* FAULT IF I'M ALWAYS SENT AGAINST *UNREASONABLE PEOPLE*.

JUST *FIND* HER.

THEN *LET* ME *WORK!*

FOLLOW THE TRACKS, AND HEY-PRESTO, A TRAVELING SHOW!

SHE'S *HERE*.

41

NEVER HAVE DONE THAT!

STOP THIS!

WHERE IS SHE?!

I— I— I— AH—

LISTEN TO ME!

THAT *ISN'T* WHAT HAPPENED!

WHO GAVE *YOU* PERMISSION TO—

SHUT UP!

THESE ARE THE *WASTELANDS!*

WE HAVE TO BE WARY, OR WE'LL BE *DEAD!*

ABNER—HE WAS GONNA GIVE ME A *REWARD!*

SHUT UP!

"YES, WE MET HER, AND *YES,* WE SENT HER AWAY."

"FRANKLY, SHE SCARED THE *HELL* OUT OF US."

"BUT THE ATTACK BY THE CLANK HAD *NOTHING* TO DO WITH HER."

"SHE WENT EAST—"

"—IT CAME FROM THE *NORTH.*"

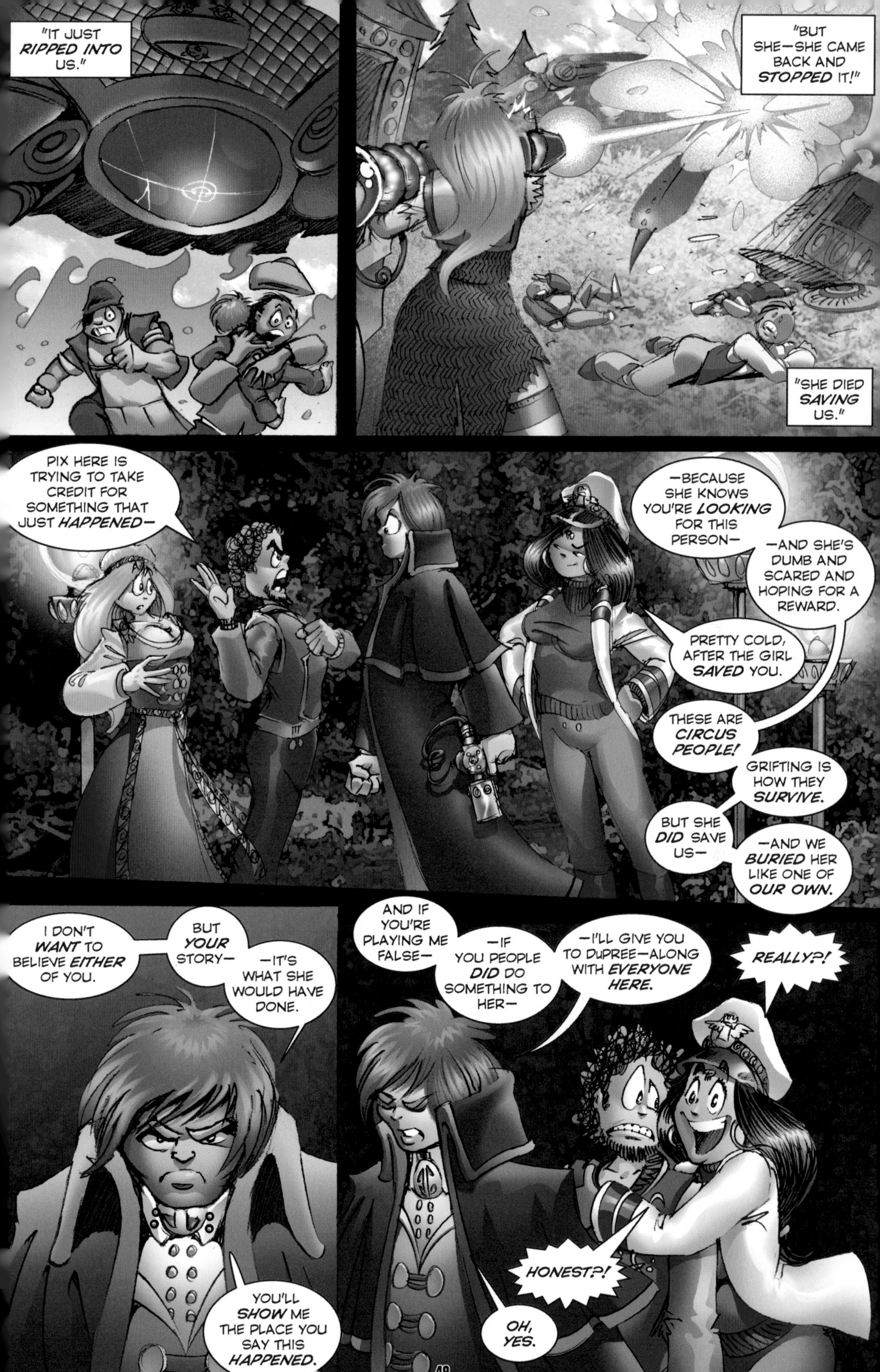
"IT JUST RIPPED INTO US."
"BUT SHE—SHE CAME BACK AND STOPPED IT!"
"SHE DIED SAVING US."
PIX HERE IS TRYING TO TAKE CREDIT FOR SOMETHING THAT JUST HAPPENED—
—BECAUSE SHE KNOWS YOU'RE LOOKING FOR THIS PERSON—
—AND SHE'S DUMB AND SCARED AND HOPING FOR A REWARD.
PRETTY COLD, AFTER THE GIRL SAVED YOU.
THESE ARE CIRCUS PEOPLE!
GRIFTING IS HOW THEY SURVIVE.
BUT SHE DID SAVE US—
—AND WE BURIED HER LIKE ONE OF OUR OWN.
I DON'T WANT TO BELIEVE EITHER OF YOU.
BUT YOUR STORY—
—IT'S WHAT SHE WOULD HAVE DONE.
YOU'LL SHOW ME THE PLACE YOU SAY THIS HAPPENED.
AND IF YOU'RE PLAYING ME FALSE—
—IF YOU PEOPLE DID DO SOMETHING TO HER—
—I'LL GIVE YOU TO DUPREE—ALONG WITH EVERYONE HERE.
REALLY?!
HONEST?!
OH, YES.

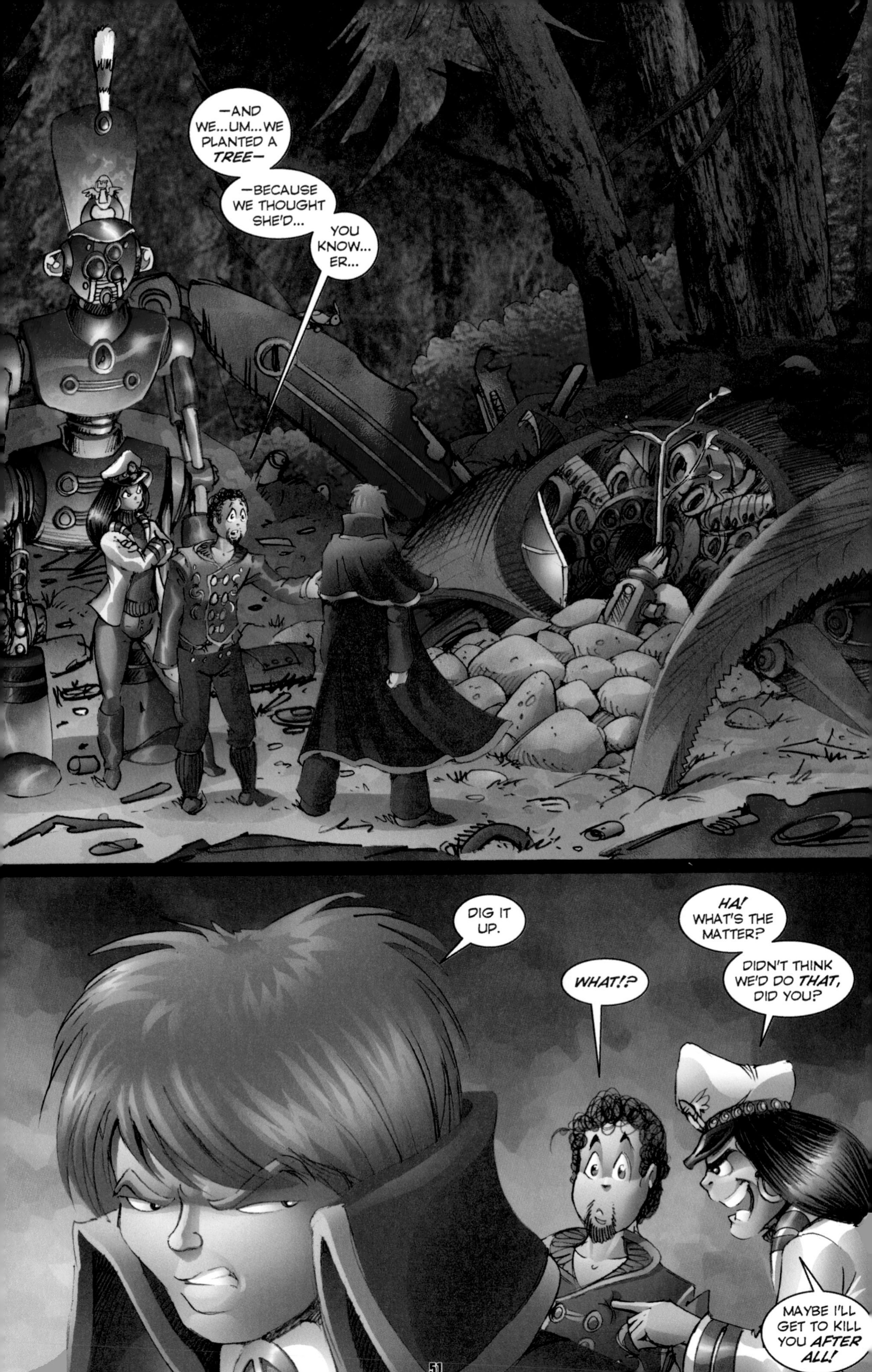
—AND WE...UM...WE PLANTED A *TREE*—
—BECAUSE WE THOUGHT SHE'D...
YOU KNOW... ER...
DIG IT UP.
WHAT!?
HA! WHAT'S THE MATTER?
DIDN'T THINK WE'D DO *THAT,* DID YOU?
MAYBE I'LL GET TO KILL YOU *AFTER ALL!*

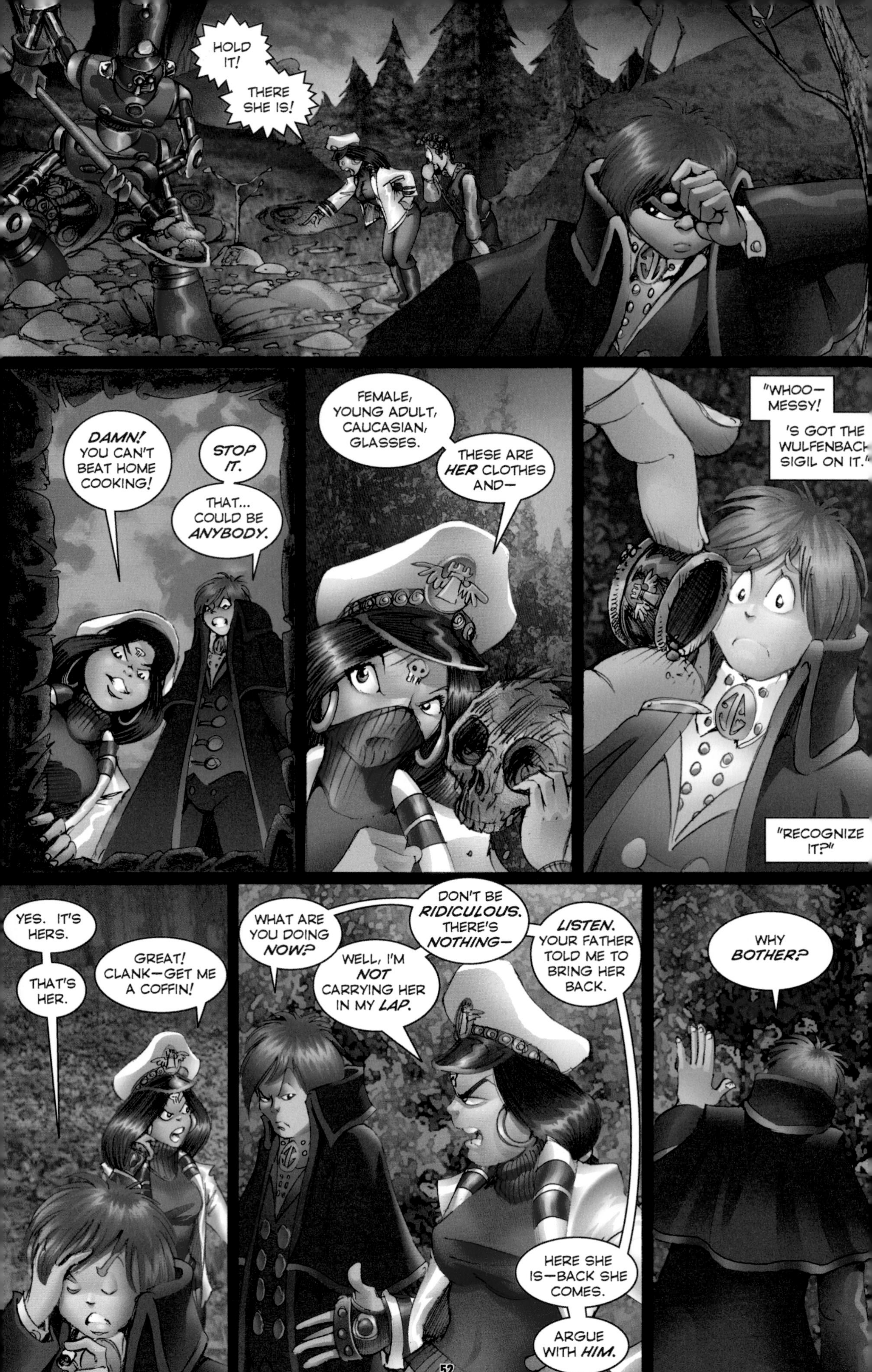
HOLD IT!
THERE SHE IS!
DAMN! YOU CAN'T BEAT HOME COOKING!
STOP IT.
THAT... COULD BE *ANYBODY.*
FEMALE, YOUNG ADULT, CAUCASIAN, GLASSES.
THESE ARE *HER* CLOTHES AND—
"WHOO—MESSY!
'S GOT THE WULFENBACH SIGIL ON IT."
"RECOGNIZE IT?"
YES. IT'S HERS.
THAT'S HER.
GREAT! CLANK—GET ME A COFFIN!
WHAT ARE YOU DOING *NOW?*
WELL, I'M *NOT* CARRYING HER IN MY *LAP.*
DON'T BE *RIDICULOUS.* THERE'S *NOTHING—*
LISTEN. YOUR FATHER TOLD ME TO BRING HER BACK.
HERE SHE IS—BACK SHE COMES.
ARGUE WITH *HIM.*
WHY *BOTHER?*

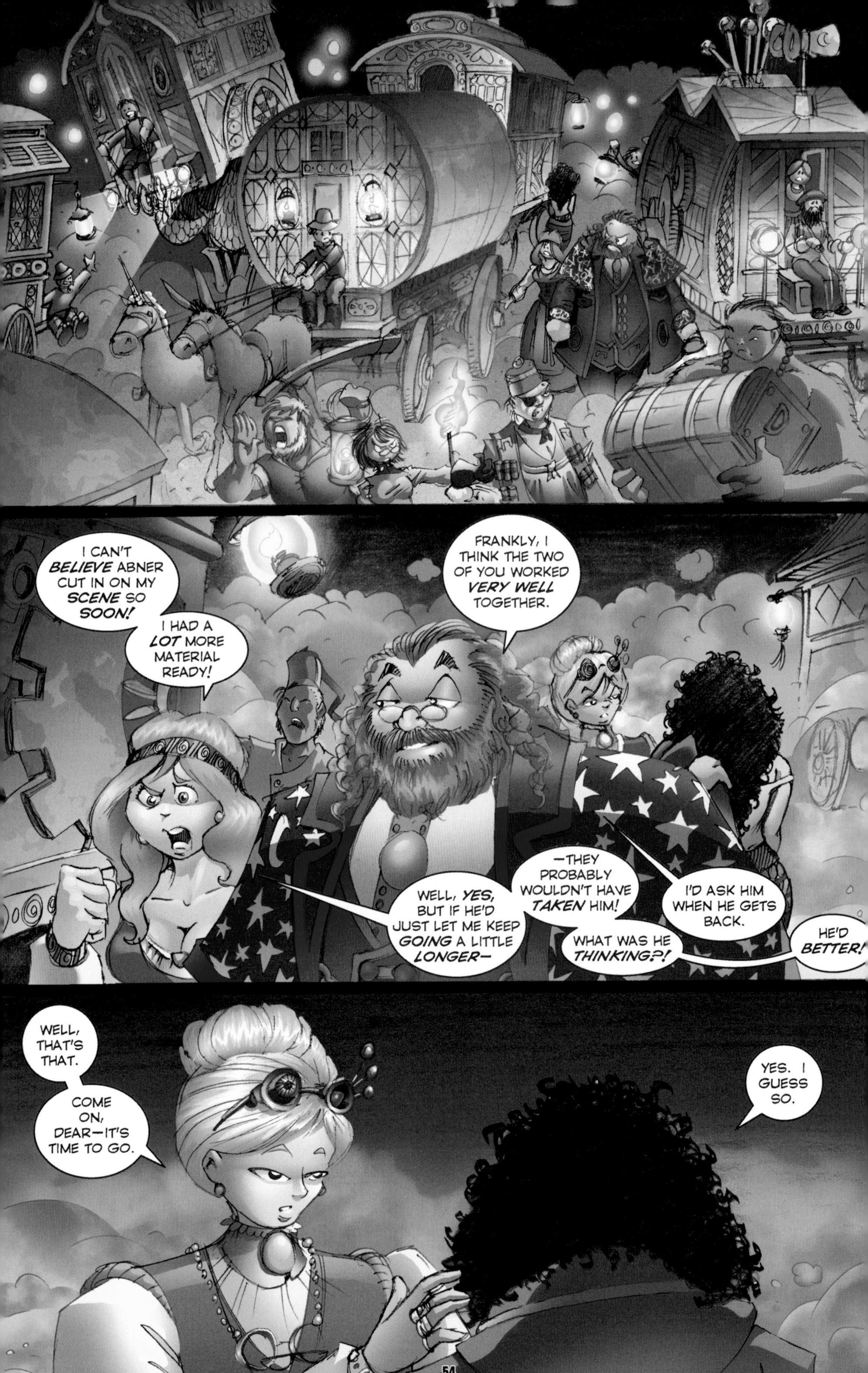
I CAN'T BELIEVE ABNER CUT IN ON MY SCENE SO SOON!
I HAD A LOT MORE MATERIAL READY!
FRANKLY, I THINK THE TWO OF YOU WORKED VERY WELL TOGETHER.
WELL, YES, BUT IF HE'D JUST LET ME KEEP GOING A LITTLE LONGER—
—THEY PROBABLY WOULDN'T HAVE TAKEN HIM!
WHAT WAS HE THINKING?!
I'D ASK HIM WHEN HE GETS BACK.
HE'D BETTER!
WELL, THAT'S THAT.
COME ON, DEAR—IT'S TIME TO GO.
YES. I GUESS SO.

"OLGA WAS NEVER HAPPIER THAN WHEN SHE'D PULLED A REALLY CLEVER SCAM—OR CONVINCED SOME TOWNIE THAT SHE WAS A CONSTRUCT—"

AND NOW? NOW SHE GETS TO FOOL NOT JUST SOME GULLIBLE *TOWNIE*—

—BUT BARON WULFENBACH *HIMSELF!*

"—OR A GRAND DUCHESS, OR AN EXPLORER FROM THE MOON. SHE *LOVED* THAT SORT OF THING."

IF SHE WEREN'T DEAD,

SHE'D HAVE *KILLED* HERSELF TO PLAY THIS PART.

SHOW PEOPLE ARE VERY STRANGE.

YOU'LL GET USED TO IT.

THAT'S WHAT *WORRIES* ME.

SO THAT WAS *ACTING*, WAS IT?

IT'S *STUPID*. YOU STILL *SMELLED* THE SAME.

I DON'T THINK HE NOTICED.

WELL— HE'S AN *IDIOT*.

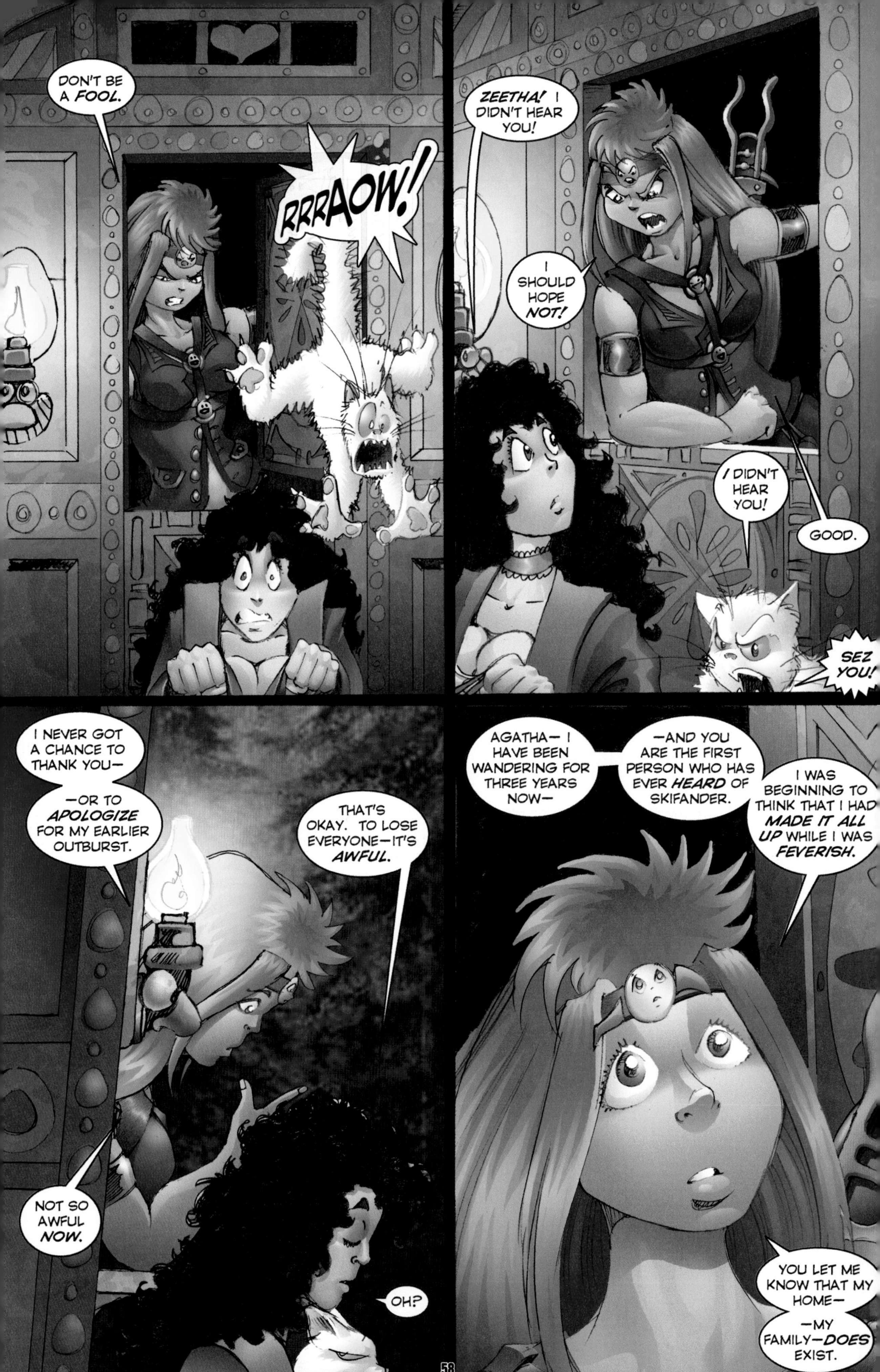
DON'T BE A FOOL.
RRRAOW!!
ZEETHA! I DIDN'T HEAR YOU!
I SHOULD HOPE NOT!
I DIDN'T HEAR YOU!
GOOD.
SEZ YOU!
I NEVER GOT A CHANCE TO THANK YOU—
—OR TO APOLOGIZE FOR MY EARLIER OUTBURST.
THAT'S OKAY. TO LOSE EVERYONE—IT'S AWFUL.
NOT SO AWFUL NOW.
OH?
AGATHA— I HAVE BEEN WANDERING FOR THREE YEARS NOW—
—AND YOU ARE THE FIRST PERSON WHO HAS EVER HEARD OF SKIFANDER.
I WAS BEGINNING TO THINK THAT I HAD MADE IT ALL UP WHILE I WAS FEVERISH.
YOU LET ME KNOW THAT MY HOME—
—MY FAMILY—DOES EXIST.

DUPREE.

WHEN I SAY THE WORDS *"ALIVE AND UNHARMED"*—

—DO *ANY* NEURONS ACTUALLY *FIRE* IN THAT BRAIN OF YOURS?

UM— NO SIR!

I THOUGHT NOT.

BUT I CAN'T TAKE CREDIT FOR THIS ONE.

SOME OLD SPIDER CLANK BURNED HER DOWN BEFORE WE GOT TO HER.

I SAVED YOU THE SIGIL PLATE.

I GOT WOOD!

HI MR. EMBI! HI MISS AGATHA!

HELLO, BALTHAZAR!

ONE MORE LOAD AND YOU'RE DONE FOR THE DAY, LADS.

AND IT LOOKS LIKE *YOU'RE* DONE NOW, AGATHA. THANK YOU.

CLANK CLANK CLANK

SO WHERE DID YOUR FAMILY GET THIS CLANK?

DAD WAS A SMITH FOR THE GILDED DUKE.

AFTER BARON WULFENBACH BEAT HIM—

—DAD TOOK SMILIN' STEV HERE AS HIS BACK PAY.

HE'S PRETTY SIMPLE.

JUST PULLS OUR CART AND FETCHES WOOD AND WATER.

SEE, THAT'S WHAT CONFUSES ME.

HUH?

THESE JOINTS ARE SO COMPLEX.

I'D HAVE SWORN THAT THIS WAS A MUCH MORE SOPHISTICATED MECHANISM.

REALLY?

WELL, DADDY SAYS STEV IS BIG AND SLOW AND STUPID—

—JUST LIKE MAMA LIKES 'EM.

WHAT?!

DADDY PLAYS PUNCH A LOT.

OH. RIGHT.

CLANK CLANK CLANK

69

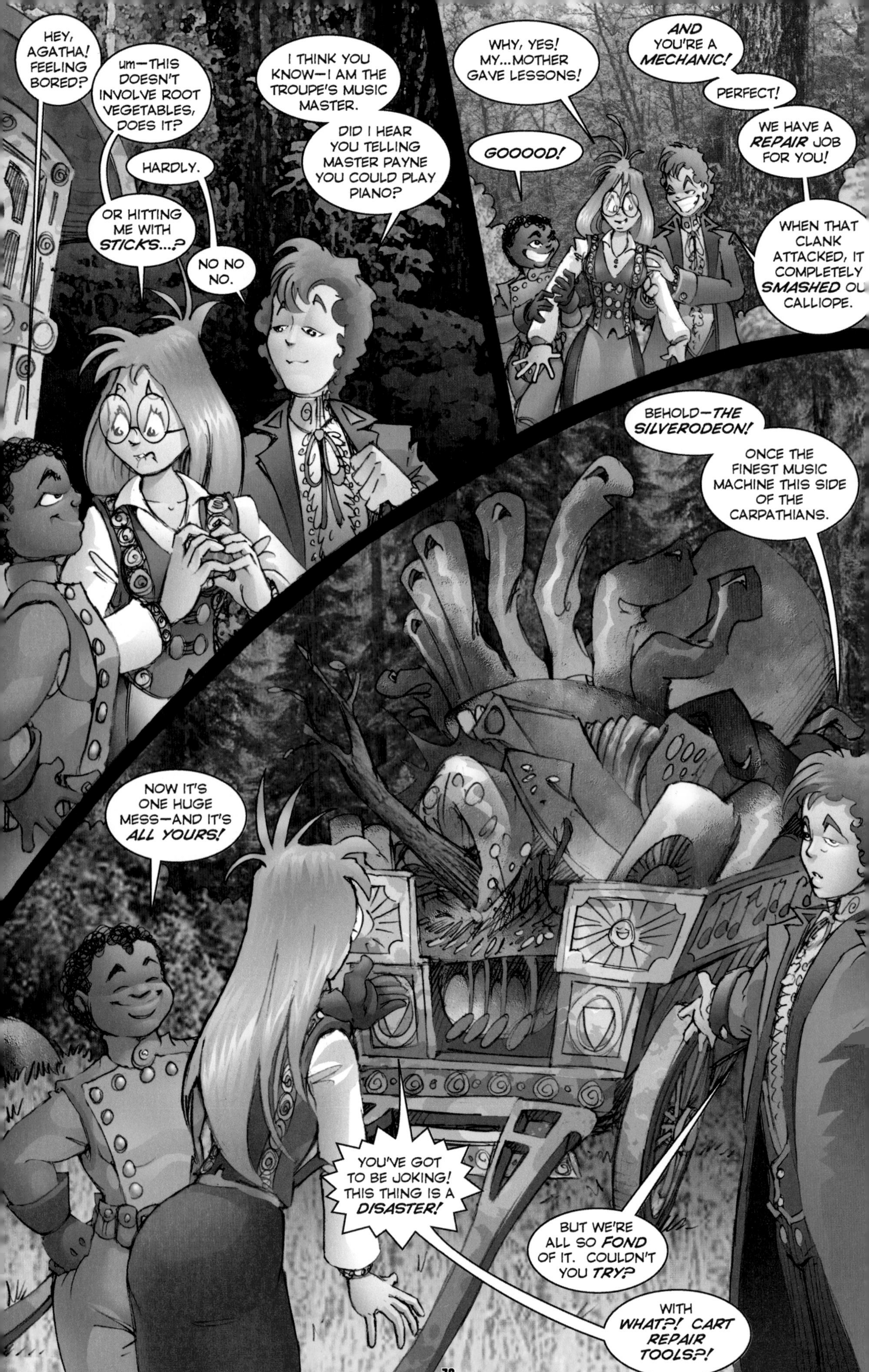
HEY, AGATHA! FEELING BORED?
um—THIS DOESN'T INVOLVE ROOT VEGETABLES, DOES IT?
HARDLY.
OR HITTING ME WITH STICKS...?
NO NO NO.
I THINK YOU KNOW—I AM THE TROUPE'S MUSIC MASTER.
DID I HEAR YOU TELLING MASTER PAYNE YOU COULD PLAY PIANO?
WHY, YES! MY...MOTHER GAVE LESSONS!
GOOOOD!
AND YOU'RE A MECHANIC!
PERFECT!
WE HAVE A REPAIR JOB FOR YOU!
WHEN THAT CLANK ATTACKED, IT COMPLETELY SMASHED OU CALLIOPE.
BEHOLD—THE SILVERODEON!
ONCE THE FINEST MUSIC MACHINE THIS SIDE OF THE CARPATHIANS.
NOW IT'S ONE HUGE MESS—AND IT'S ALL YOURS!
YOU'VE GOT TO BE JOKING! THIS THING IS A DISASTER!
BUT WE'RE ALL SO FOND OF IT. COULDN'T YOU TRY?
WITH WHAT?! CART REPAIR TOOLS?!

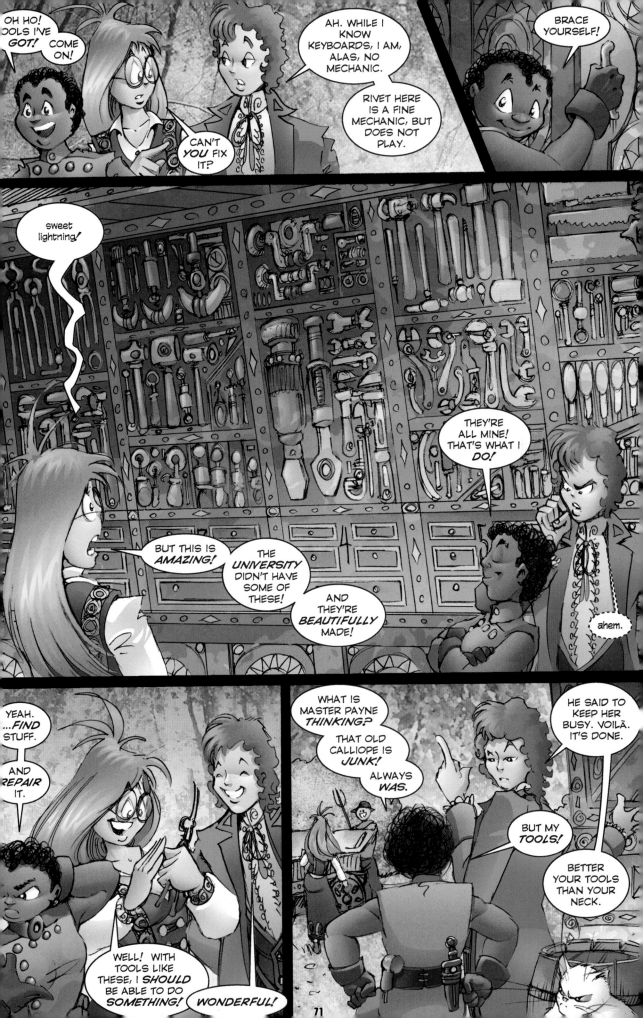

OH HO! TOOLS I'VE **GOT!** COME ON!

CAN'T **YOU** FIX IT?

AH. WHILE I KNOW KEYBOARDS, I AM, ALAS, NO MECHANIC.

RIVET HERE IS A FINE MECHANIC, BUT DOES NOT PLAY.

BRACE YOURSELF!

sweet lightning!

THEY'RE ALL MINE! THAT'S WHAT I **DO!**

BUT THIS IS **AMAZING!**

THE **UNIVERSITY** DIDN'T HAVE SOME OF THESE!

AND THEY'RE **BEAUTIFULLY** MADE!

ahem.

YEAH. ...**FIND** STUFF.

AND **REPAIR** IT.

WELL! WITH TOOLS LIKE THESE, I **SHOULD** BE ABLE TO DO **SOMETHING!**

WONDERFUL!

WHAT IS MASTER PAYNE **THINKING?**

THAT OLD CALLIOPE IS **JUNK!** ALWAYS **WAS.**

HE SAID TO KEEP HER BUSY. VOILÀ. IT'S DONE.

BUT MY **TOOLS!**

BETTER YOUR TOOLS THAN YOUR NECK.

71

HEY, THERE'S *ALWAYS* SOMETHING OUT THERE. GIVE ME *SOME* CREDIT.

I RODE DOWNSTREAM FOR ABOUT TWO KILOMETERS.

SORRY, AB—IT'S MY JOB.

HE LOOKS PRETTY HUNGRY TO ME.

YEAH—WE'LL FATTEN HIM UP BEFORE HE PULLS ANYTHING. C'MON LET'S SEE THOSE TEETH!

UMF! CLOSEMOUTHED BEAST!

ABNER!

PIX.

ARE...ARE YOU ALL RIGHT?

WELL...WELL GOOD. SO—UM—

SO—

I AM.

—SO WHAT'S THE IDEA OF HORNING IN ON MY ACT, HEY?

I HAD TO!

I THOUGHT HE WAS GOING TO *KILL* YOU!

OH NO—I DON'T THINK SO. HE DIDN'T STRIKE ME AS THE TYPE TO SHOOT AN UNARMED GIRL.

HE WAS JUST MAKING A LOT OF NOISE. I HAD HIM PRETTY RATTLED, AFTER ALL.

BUT IT *WOULD* HAVE HELPED TO HAVE KNOWN—

—THAT IT WAS A *LOVER* COMING AFTER YOU, AGATHA.

WE ALL THOUGHT THEY WERE LOOKING FOR YOU BECAUSE YOU'D *STOLEN* SOMETHING!

BUT I—HE'S *NOT*—

73

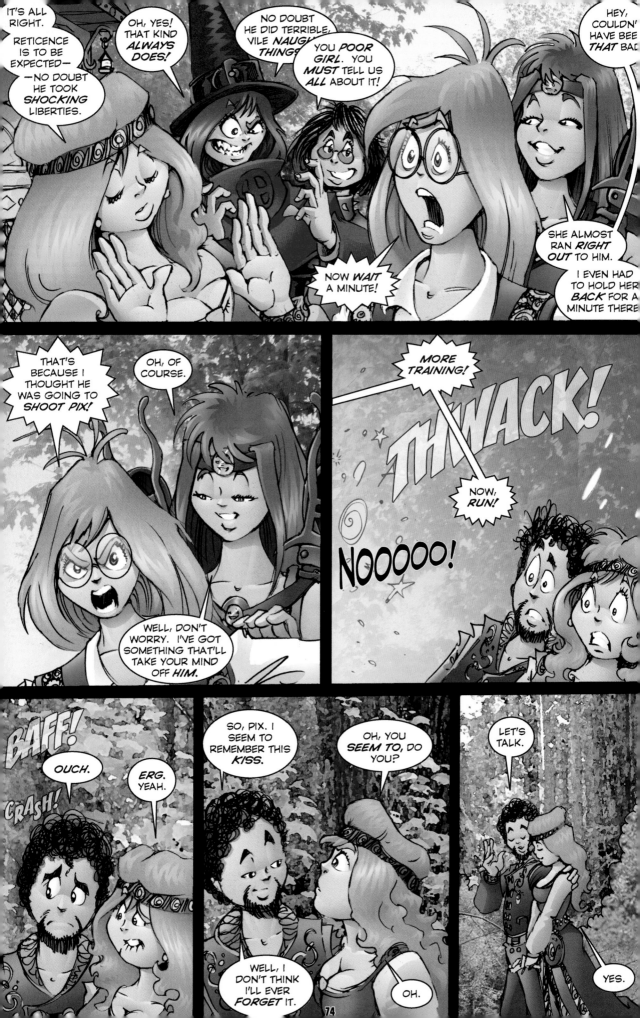

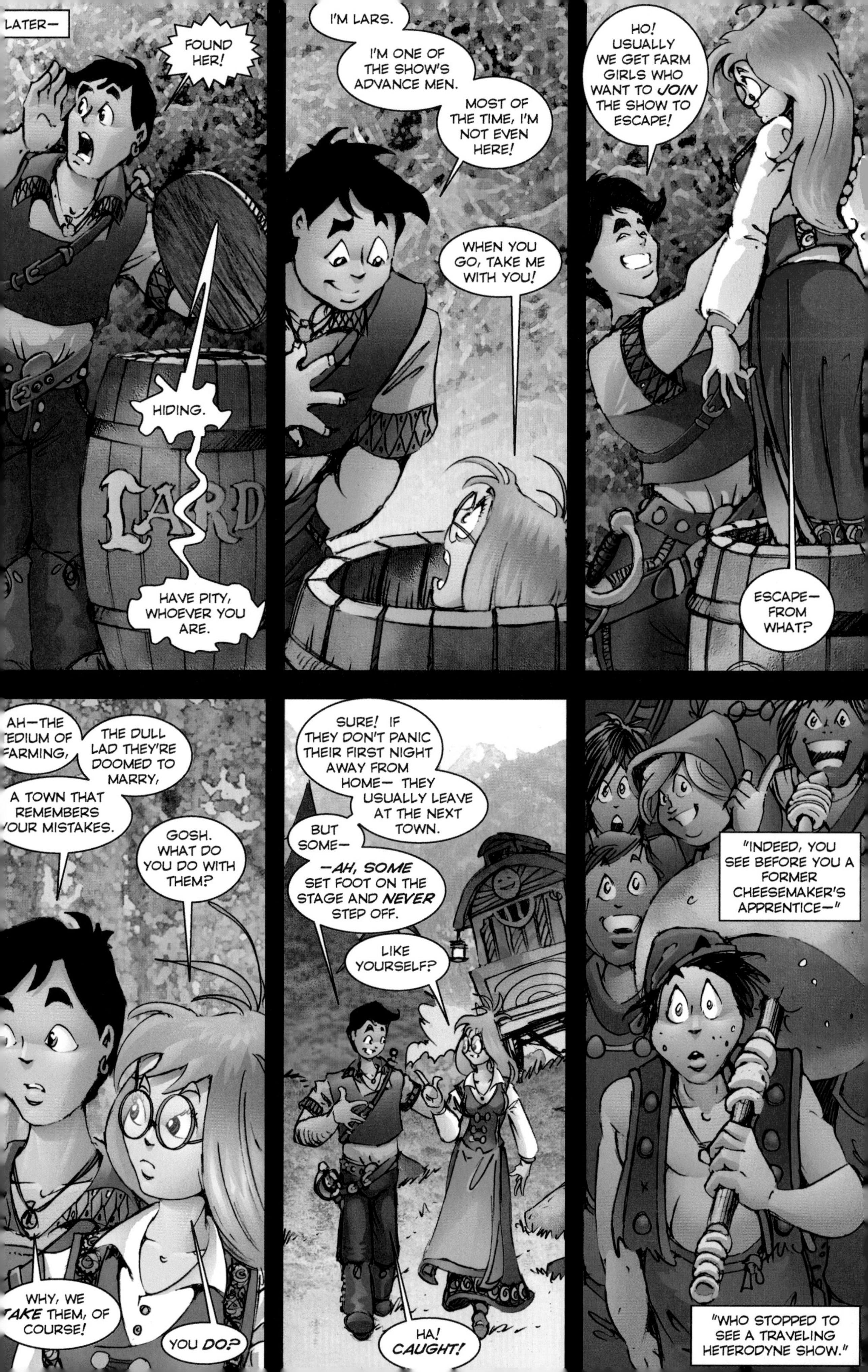
LATER—
FOUND HER!
HIDING.
HAVE PITY, WHOEVER YOU ARE.
I'M LARS.
I'M ONE OF THE SHOW'S ADVANCE MEN.
MOST OF THE TIME, I'M NOT EVEN HERE!
WHEN YOU GO, TAKE ME WITH YOU!
HO! USUALLY WE GET FARM GIRLS WHO WANT TO *JOIN* THE SHOW TO ESCAPE!
ESCAPE—FROM WHAT?
AH—THE TEDIUM OF FARMING,
THE DULL LAD THEY'RE DOOMED TO MARRY,
A TOWN THAT REMEMBERS YOUR MISTAKES.
GOSH. WHAT DO YOU DO WITH THEM?
WHY, WE *TAKE* THEM, OF COURSE!
YOU *DO?*
SURE! IF THEY DON'T PANIC THEIR FIRST NIGHT AWAY FROM HOME— THEY USUALLY LEAVE AT THE NEXT TOWN.
BUT SOME—
—*AH, SOME* SET FOOT ON THE STAGE AND *NEVER* STEP OFF.
LIKE YOURSELF?
HA! *CAUGHT!*
"INDEED, YOU SEE BEFORE YOU A FORMER CHEESEMAKER'S APPRENTICE—"
"WHO STOPPED TO SEE A TRAVELING HETERODYNE SHOW."

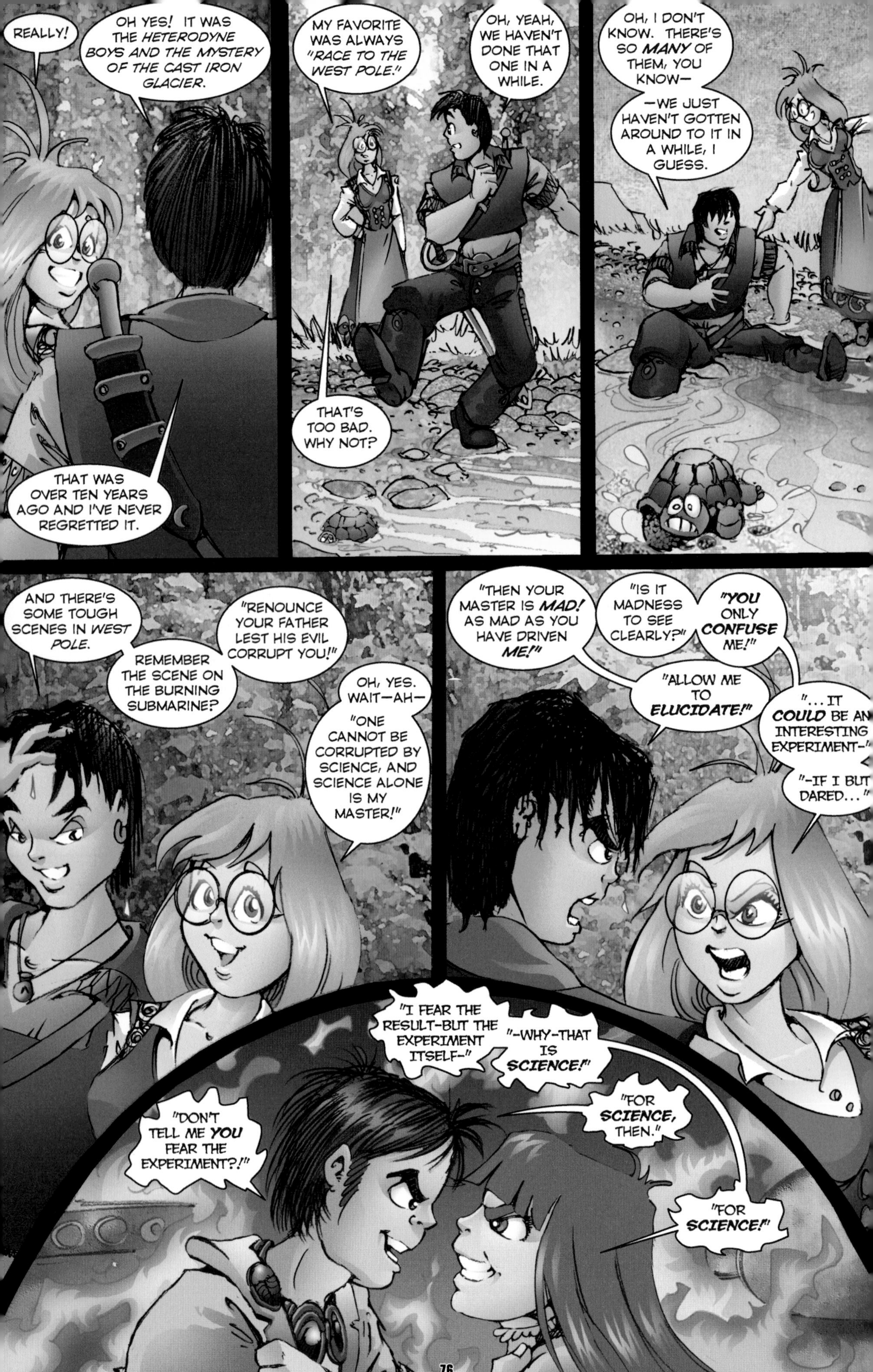
REALLY!
OH YES! IT WAS THE HETERODYNE BOYS AND THE MYSTERY OF THE CAST IRON GLACIER.
THAT WAS OVER TEN YEARS AGO AND I'VE NEVER REGRETTED IT.
MY FAVORITE WAS ALWAYS "RACE TO THE WEST POLE."
OH, YEAH, WE HAVEN'T DONE THAT ONE IN A WHILE.
THAT'S TOO BAD. WHY NOT?
OH, I DON'T KNOW. THERE'S SO MANY OF THEM, YOU KNOW—
—WE JUST HAVEN'T GOTTEN AROUND TO IT IN A WHILE, I GUESS.
AND THERE'S SOME TOUGH SCENES IN WEST POLE.
REMEMBER THE SCENE ON THE BURNING SUBMARINE?
"RENOUNCE YOUR FATHER LEST HIS EVIL CORRUPT YOU!"
OH, YES. WAIT—AH—
"ONE CANNOT BE CORRUPTED BY SCIENCE, AND SCIENCE ALONE IS MY MASTER!"
"THEN YOUR MASTER IS MAD! AS MAD AS YOU HAVE DRIVEN ME!"
"IS IT MADNESS TO SEE CLEARLY?"
"YOU ONLY CONFUSE ME!"
"ALLOW ME TO ELUCIDATE!"
"... IT COULD BE AN INTERESTING EXPERIMENT-"
"-IF I BUT DARED..."
"I FEAR THE RESULT-BUT THE EXPERIMENT ITSELF-"
"-WHY-THAT IS SCIENCE!"
"DON'T TELL ME YOU FEAR THE EXPERIMENT?!"
"FOR SCIENCE, THEN."
"FOR SCIENCE!"

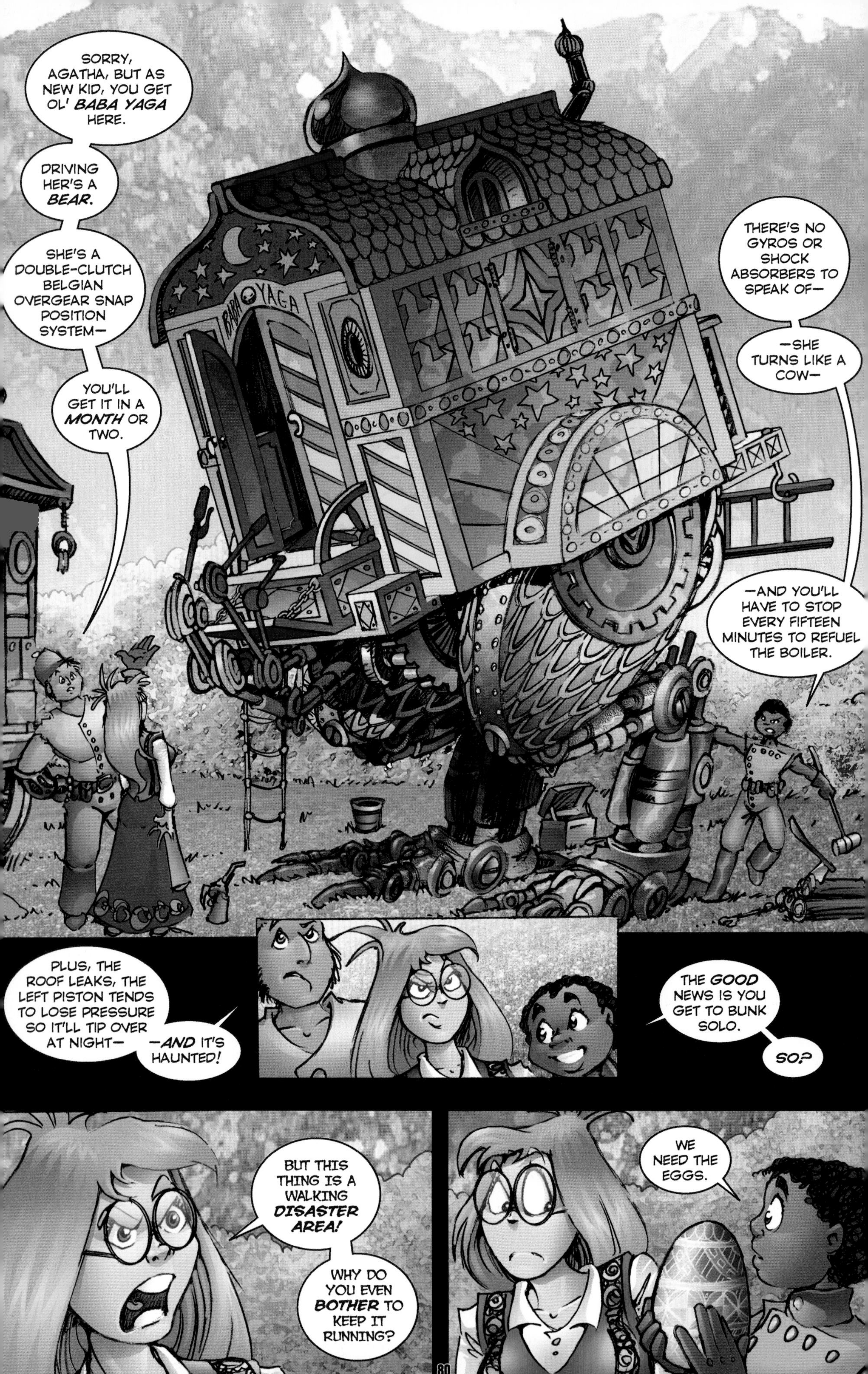
SORRY, AGATHA, BUT AS NEW KID, YOU GET OL' *BABA YAGA* HERE.
DRIVING HER'S A *BEAR.*
SHE'S A DOUBLE-CLUTCH BELGIAN OVERGEAR SNAP POSITION SYSTEM—
YOU'LL GET IT IN A *MONTH* OR TWO.
BABA YAGA
THERE'S NO GYROS OR SHOCK ABSORBERS TO SPEAK OF—
—SHE TURNS LIKE A COW—
—AND YOU'LL HAVE TO STOP EVERY FIFTEEN MINUTES TO REFUEL THE BOILER.
PLUS, THE ROOF LEAKS, THE LEFT PISTON TENDS TO LOSE PRESSURE SO IT'LL TIP OVER AT NIGHT—
—AND IT'S HAUNTED!
THE *GOOD* NEWS IS YOU GET TO BUNK SOLO.
SO?
BUT THIS THING IS A WALKING *DISASTER AREA!*
WHY DO YOU EVEN *BOTHER* TO KEEP IT RUNNING?
WE NEED THE EGGS.

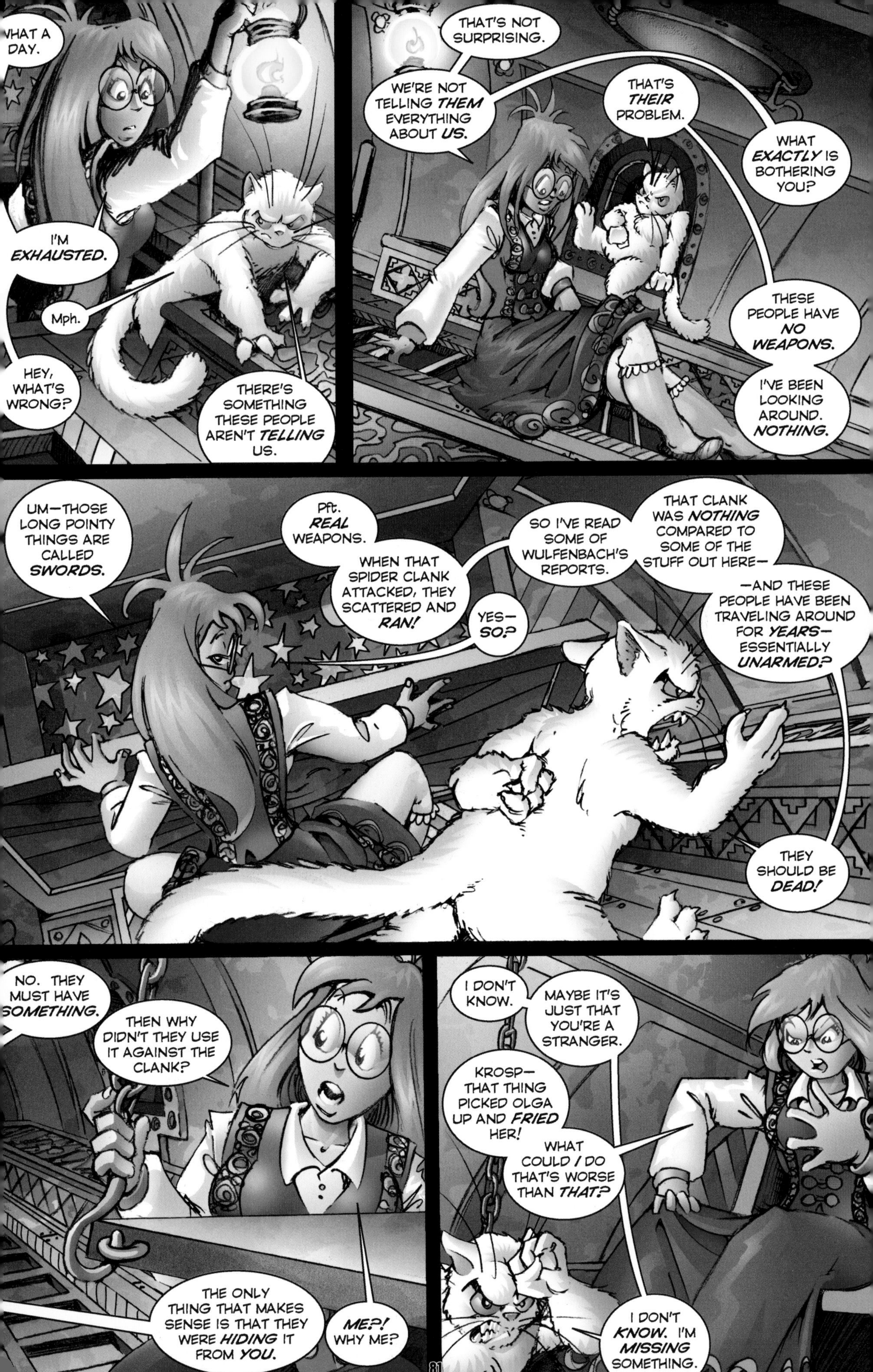
WHAT A DAY.
I'M EXHAUSTED.
Mph.
HEY, WHAT'S WRONG?
THERE'S SOMETHING THESE PEOPLE AREN'T TELLING US.
THAT'S NOT SURPRISING.
WE'RE NOT TELLING THEM EVERYTHING ABOUT US.
THAT'S THEIR PROBLEM.
WHAT EXACTLY IS BOTHERING YOU?
THESE PEOPLE HAVE NO WEAPONS.
I'VE BEEN LOOKING AROUND. NOTHING.
UM—THOSE LONG POINTY THINGS ARE CALLED SWORDS.
Pft. REAL WEAPONS.
WHEN THAT SPIDER CLANK ATTACKED, THEY SCATTERED AND RAN!
YES— SO?
SO I'VE READ SOME OF WULFENBACH'S REPORTS.
THAT CLANK WAS NOTHING COMPARED TO SOME OF THE STUFF OUT HERE—
—AND THESE PEOPLE HAVE BEEN TRAVELING AROUND FOR YEARS— ESSENTIALLY UNARMED?
THEY SHOULD BE DEAD!
NO. THEY MUST HAVE SOMETHING.
THEN WHY DIDN'T THEY USE IT AGAINST THE CLANK?
THE ONLY THING THAT MAKES SENSE IS THAT THEY WERE HIDING IT FROM YOU.
ME?! WHY ME?
I DON'T KNOW.
MAYBE IT'S JUST THAT YOU'RE A STRANGER.
KROSP— THAT THING PICKED OLGA UP AND FRIED HER!
WHAT COULD I DO THAT'S WORSE THAN THAT?
I DON'T KNOW. I'M MISSING SOMETHING.

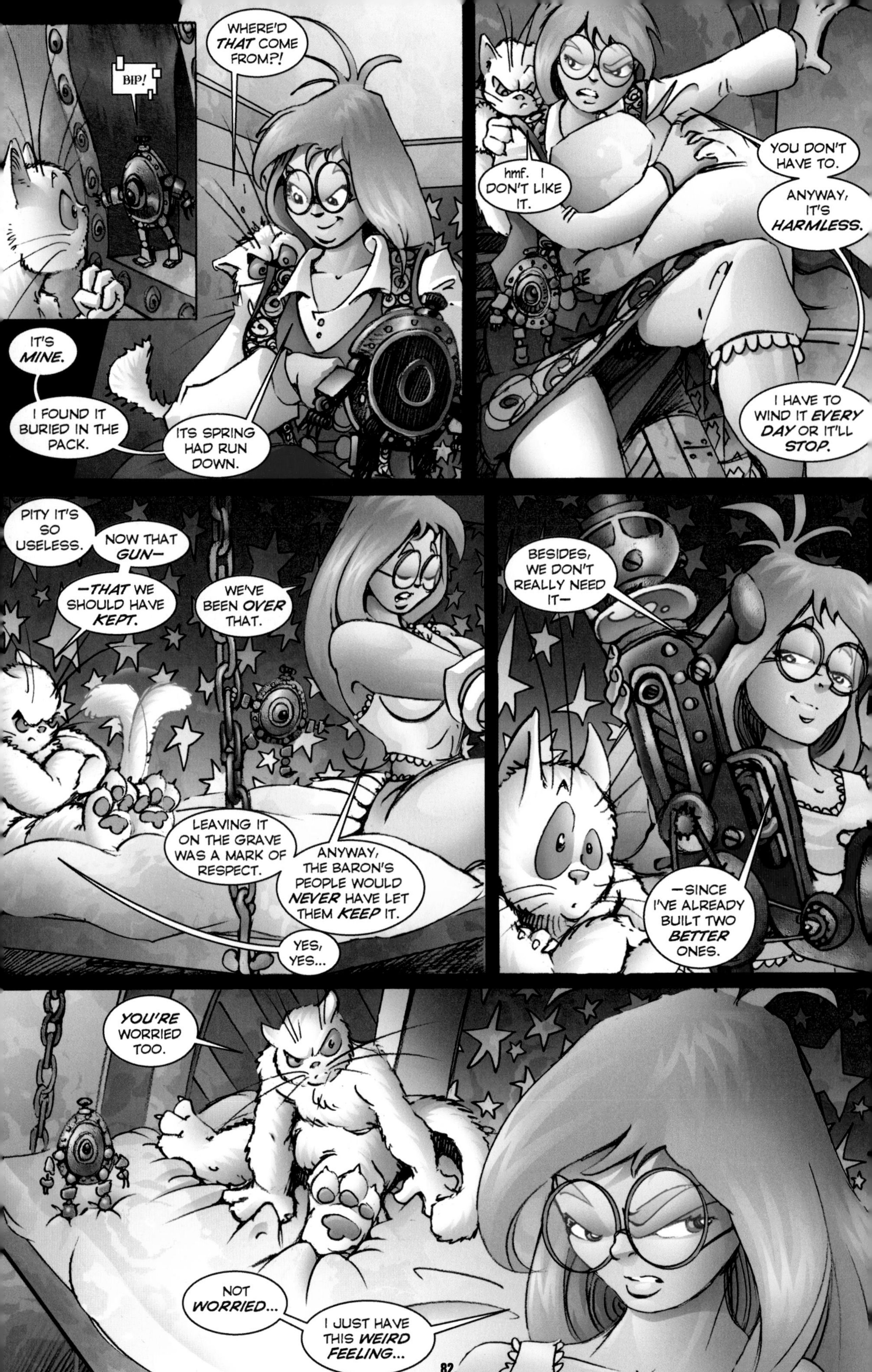
BIP!
WHERE'D THAT COME FROM?!
IT'S MINE.
I FOUND IT BURIED IN THE PACK.
ITS SPRING HAD RUN DOWN.
hmf. I DON'T LIKE IT.
YOU DON'T HAVE TO.
ANYWAY, IT'S HARMLESS.
I HAVE TO WIND IT EVERY DAY OR IT'LL STOP.
PITY IT'S SO USELESS.
NOW THAT GUN—
—THAT WE SHOULD HAVE KEPT.
WE'VE BEEN OVER THAT.
LEAVING IT ON THE GRAVE WAS A MARK OF RESPECT.
ANYWAY, THE BARON'S PEOPLE WOULD NEVER HAVE LET THEM KEEP IT.
YES, YES...
BESIDES, WE DON'T REALLY NEED IT—
—SINCE I'VE ALREADY BUILT TWO BETTER ONES.
YOU'RE WORRIED TOO.
NOT WORRIED...
I JUST HAVE THIS WEIRD FEELING...

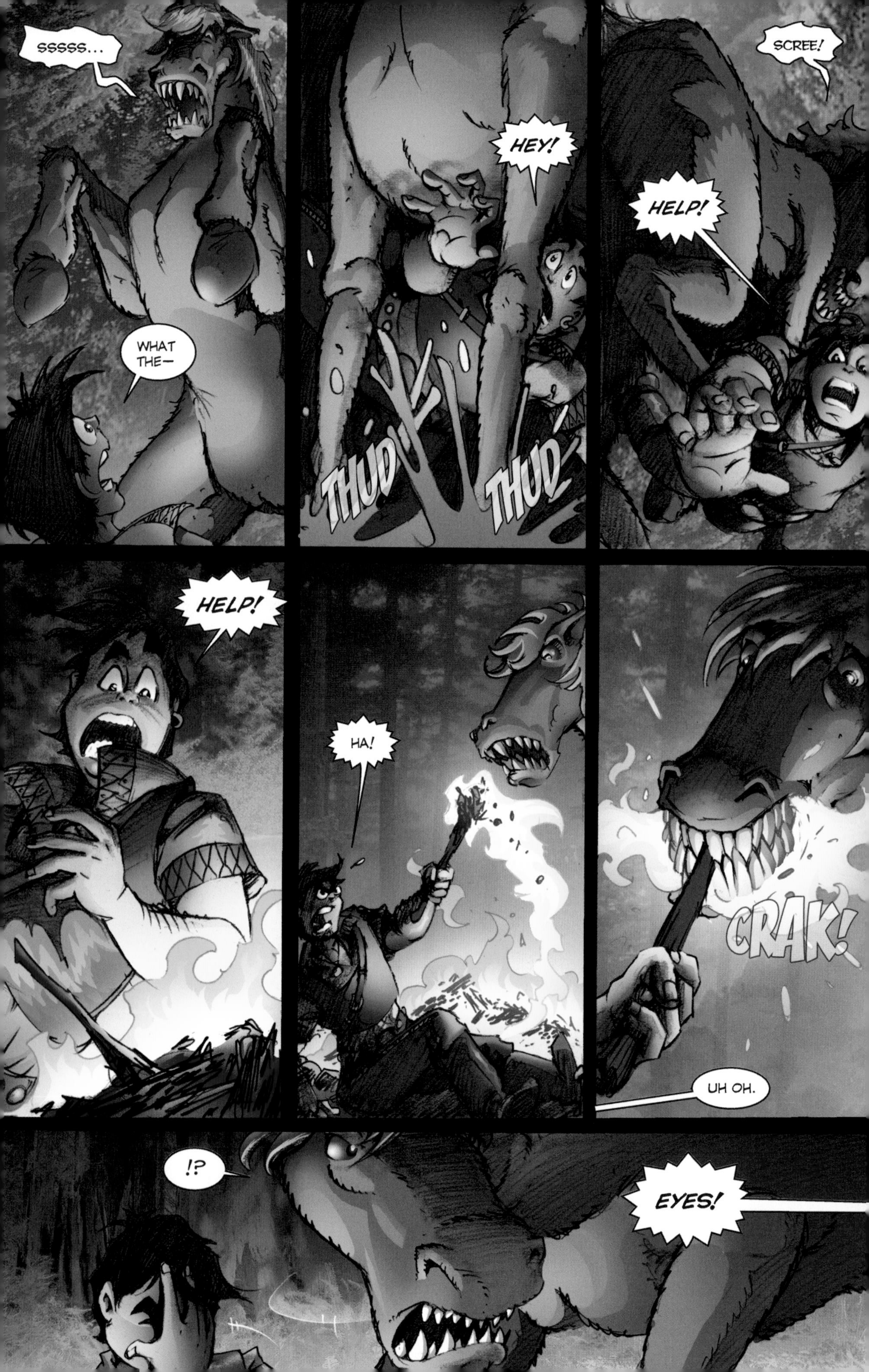
SSSSS...
WHAT THE—
HEY!
THUD
THUD
SCREE!
HELP!
HELP!
HA!
CRAK!
UH OH.
!?
EYES!

PWHAM!

COVER YOUR EARS! I'M USING THE SONIC GUN!

EEEEE!

AUT VINCERE AUT MORI!

chok!

I'M POWERING UP THE GRAVITY ENGINE!

OOOMMMM

NONE OF THAT IS WORKING! I'M RELEASING MY POISONOUS SKY WYRMS!

ZZZ

NO!

ZZZZZZZZZZZZZZZZZ

FWHAAAARR!

IT BREATHES FIRE?!

OH! THAT'S CHEATING! IT'S NOT FAIR!

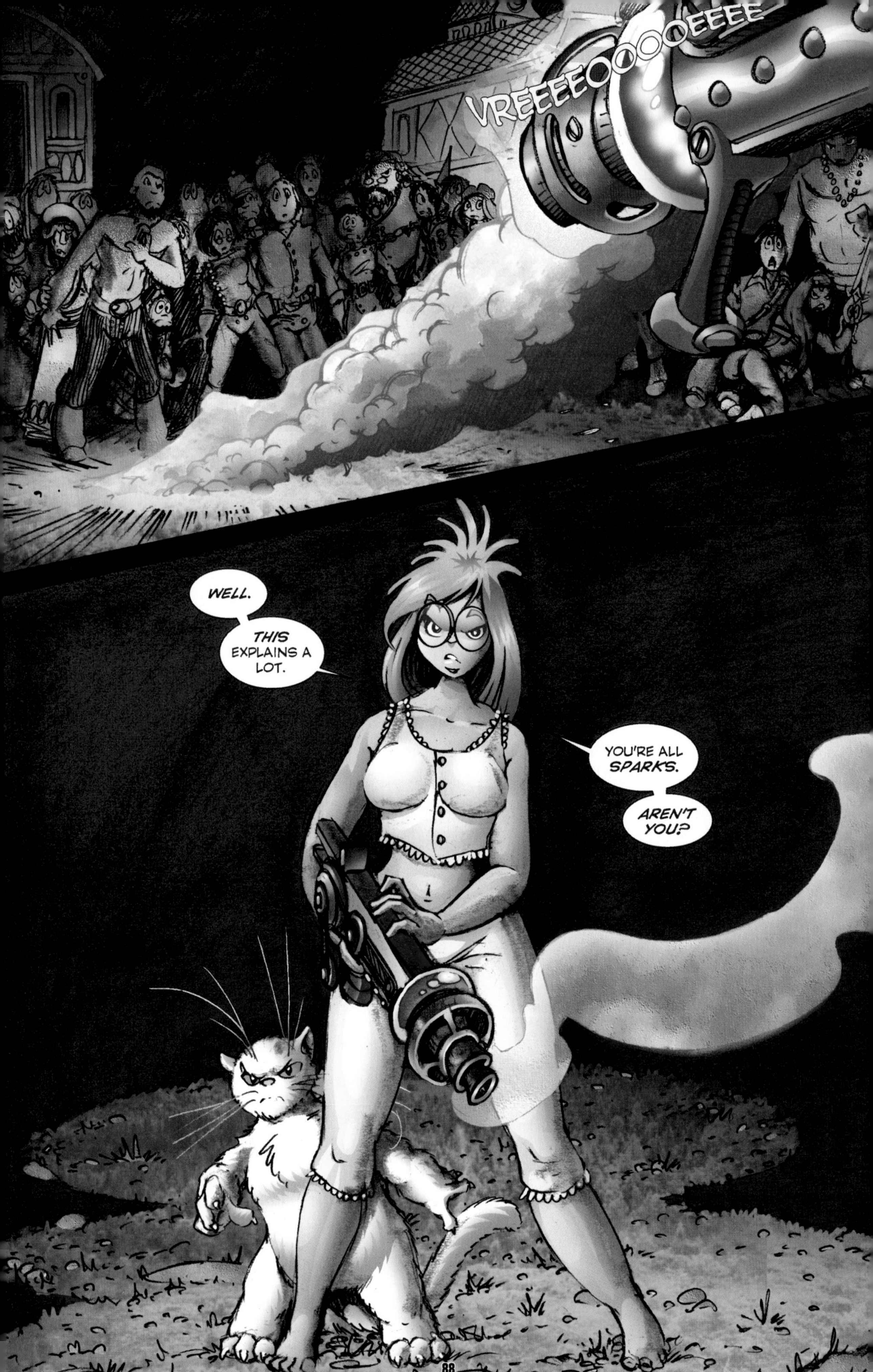
VREEEEOOOOOEEEE
WELL.
THIS EXPLAINS A LOT.
YOU'RE ALL SPARKS.
AREN'T YOU?

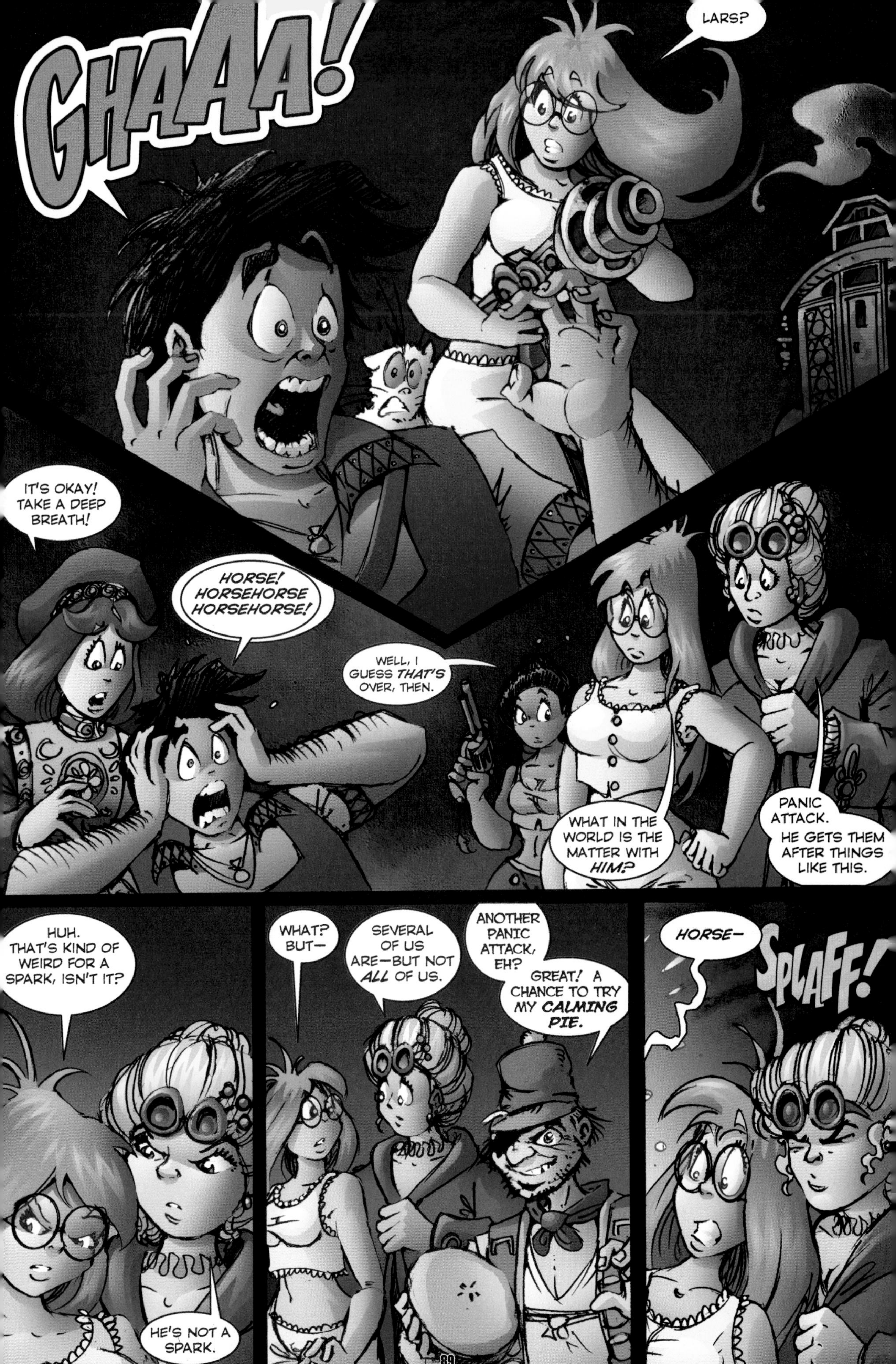
GHAAA!
LARS?
IT'S OKAY! TAKE A DEEP BREATH!
HORSE! HORSEHORSE HORSEHORSE!
WELL, I GUESS THAT'S OVER, THEN.
WHAT IN THE WORLD IS THE MATTER WITH HIM?
PANIC ATTACK.
HE GETS THEM AFTER THINGS LIKE THIS.
HUH. THAT'S KIND OF WEIRD FOR A SPARK, ISN'T IT?
HE'S NOT A SPARK.
WHAT? BUT—
SEVERAL OF US ARE—BUT NOT ALL OF US.
ANOTHER PANIC ATTACK, EH?
GREAT! A CHANCE TO TRY MY CALMING PIE.
HORSE—
SPLAFF!

SOON—

SO THE POINT IS, EVERYBODY *KNOWS* WHAT THE *SPARK* IS—RIGHT??

JUST ASK THE PEOPLE WHO COME TO OUR SHOWS.

SO?

TO THEM, "THE SPARK" MEANS YOU'RE ANOTHER LIKE WULFENBACH, OR THE HETERODYNES.

EXCEPT IT DOESN'T ALWAYS *WORK* LIKE THAT.

"WHAT ABOUT SOMEONE REALLY BRILLIANT, BUT BORN INTO A POOR VILLAGE?"

"WITHOUT ANY EDUCATION, WHAT CAN THEY DO?"

"AND THERE ARE... VARYING DEGREES OF TALENT."

"THE WORST OFF ARE THOSE WITH JUST ENOUGH TALENT THAT PEOPLE SAY 'AH, A SPARK'—

—BUT WITH LITTLE POWER TO PROTECT THEMSELVES."

THAT IS WHAT YOU WILL FIND HERE.

WE PLAY MADBOYS ON THE STAGE AND PERFORM MUNDANE MIRACLES."

"WE'RE JUST PLAYERS IN A SHOW, AND SO WE ARE ABLE TO HIDE IN PLAIN SIGHT."

DR. PRONI AND OLLY

"EVEN FROM THE BARON."

YOU THOUGHT *HE* HAD SENT THE SPIDER CLANK.

THE BARON OR SOMEONE LIKE HIM.

THERE ARE MANY WHO HAVE A USE FOR WEAK SPARKS.

NO!

I WANT HER TO STAY! *HER!*

I SEE. WELL, IT'S LATE, I GUESS I'D BETTER GO—

MISS CLAY? WHY?

91

BECAUSE SHE'S GOT A GREAT BIG MONSTER-KILLING GUN—

AND I WANT IT AND HER *RIGHT HERE!*

I'LL STAY.

THANK YOU, MISS CLAY. I APPRECIATE IT.

CAN'T ARGUE WITH *THAT* LOGIC.

Z

HEAVENS! HE'S ALREADY ASLEEP.

WELL! NOBODY'S HAD THAT MUCH FAITH IN ME SINCE—

Z

...SINCE?

NOTHING. NEVER MIND.

I SEE. GOOD NIGHT, THEN.

GOOD NIGHT.

IS LARS OKAY, SIR?

MM? OH, YES. MISS CLAY WILL STAY WITH HIM.

HUH. I GUESS THERE'S NO MORE DOUBT— —SHE'S A SPARK. A *STRONG* ONE, I'D GUESS.

THAT'S RIGHT.

AND ON THE RUN FROM WULFENBACH.

WELL, MOXANA'S NEW *GAME* IS MAKING MORE AND MORE SENSE.

YOU DON'T SOUND HAPPY.

WE... COULD *LOSE* HER AT THE NEXT TOWN...

NO, AB—I DON'T THINK WE COULD.

OUR TASK IS TO GET HER TO MECHANICSBURG.

WE'LL MOVE OUT IN THE MORNING.

USE ALL THE WOOD YOU NEED. I WANT THAT HORSE BURNED *TONIGHT.*

I'LL DO IT MYSELF.

GOOD LAD.

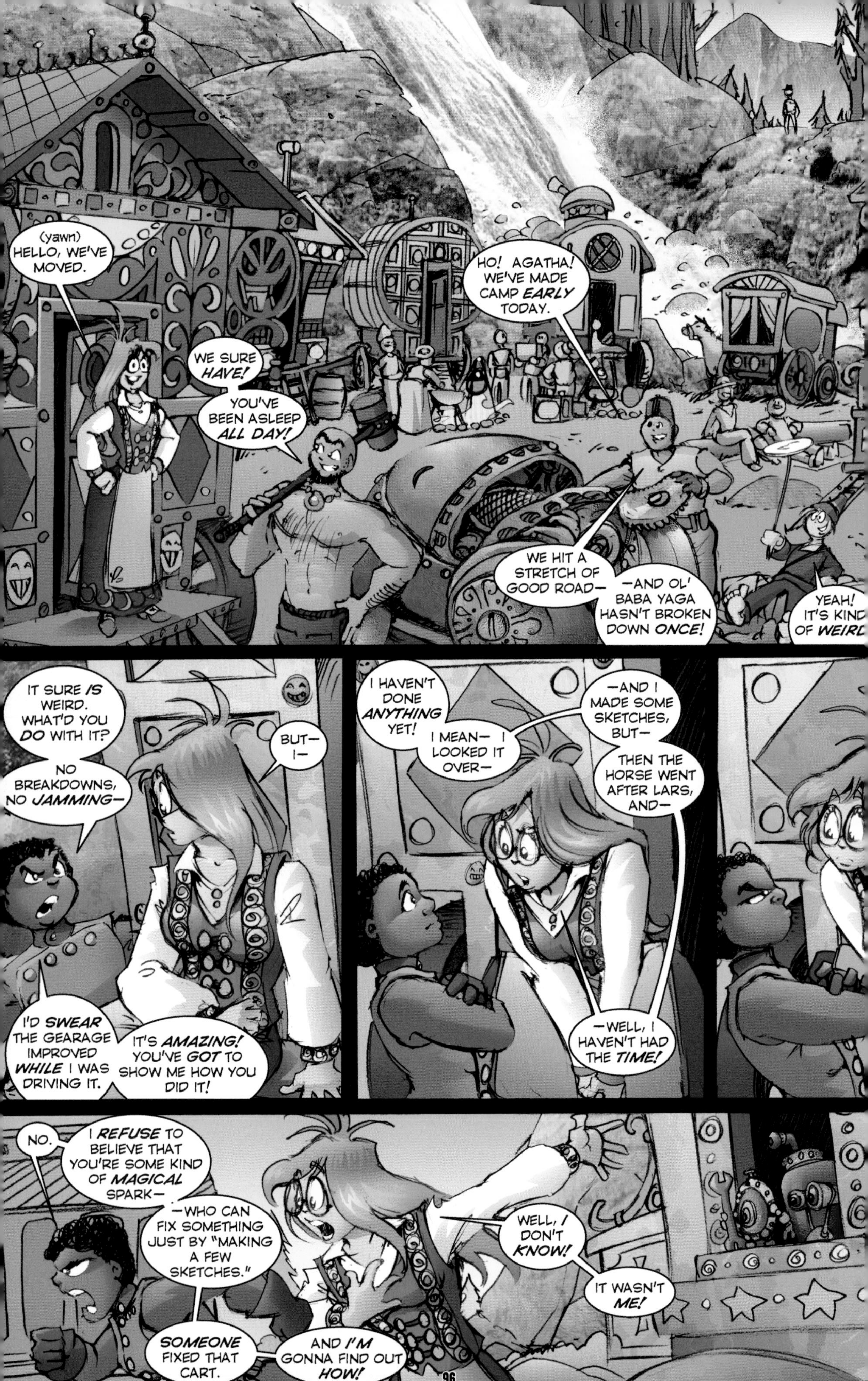

(yawn) HELLO, WE'VE MOVED.
WE SURE *HAVE!*
YOU'VE BEEN ASLEEP *ALL DAY!*
HO! AGATHA! WE'VE MADE CAMP *EARLY* TODAY.
WE HIT A STRETCH OF GOOD ROAD—
—AND OL' BABA YAGA HASN'T BROKEN DOWN *ONCE!*
YEAH! IT'S KIND OF *WEIRD*
IT SURE *IS* WEIRD. WHAT'D YOU *DO* WITH IT?
NO BREAKDOWNS, NO *JAMMING*—
BUT— I—
I'D *SWEAR* THE GEARAGE IMPROVED *WHILE* I WAS DRIVING IT.
IT'S *AMAZING!* YOU'VE *GOT* TO SHOW ME HOW YOU DID IT!
I HAVEN'T DONE *ANYTHING* YET!
I MEAN— I LOOKED IT OVER—
—AND I MADE SOME SKETCHES, BUT—
THEN THE HORSE WENT AFTER LARS, AND—
—WELL, I HAVEN'T HAD THE *TIME!*
NO.
I *REFUSE* TO BELIEVE THAT YOU'RE SOME KIND OF *MAGICAL* SPARK—
—WHO CAN FIX SOMETHING JUST BY "MAKING A FEW SKETCHES."
WELL, *I* DON'T *KNOW!*
IT WASN'T *ME!*
SOMEONE FIXED THAT CART.
AND *I'M* GONNA FIND OUT *HOW!*

WHAT'S GOING ON?

AND DAME AEDITH WILL DO HER KNIFE THROWING.

THIS TIME, DO *NOT* ASK IF THERE ARE ANY VAMPIRES IN THE AUDIENCE!

HOW WAS *I* TO KNOW THAT GUY WAS *JOKING?*

WHO'D JOKE ABOUT *VAMPIRES?!*

WE'LL BE HITTING THE TOWN OF ZUMZUM SOON.

SO THEY'RE ASSIGNING PARTS FOR THE SHOW.

SO THAT BRINGS US TO THE MAIN SHOW—

—AND THE *HETERODYNE* PLAY WE'LL BE DOING.

HOW ABOUT *THE FOG MERCHANT?* I'VE GOT SOME LADDER BUSINESS I WANT TO TRY IN SCENE 2!

TOO BAD, IT'S ALREADY DECIDED.

WE'RE DOING *RACE TO THE WEST POLE.*

OO! OO! *CLOCKWORK SUNDIAL!*

OO— HAVEN'T DONE *THAT* ONE IN A WHILE.

HOW ABOUT *THE RACING SNAILS OF DR. ZEGREB?*

BUT I THOUGHT PIX DIDN'T LIKE PLAYING LUCREZIA.

I *DON'T.* I ALWAYS WANTED TO PLAY THE *HIGH PRIESTESS.*

WHICH IS WHY *AGATHA* GETS TO PLAY LUCREZIA.

WHAT? BUT—

LARS SAID YOU'RE PRETTY GOOD—

—AND I'VE LEARNED TO TRUST HIS INSTINCTS.

BESIDES, HE PLAYS BILL AND HE'S GOOD AT ONSTAGE COACHING.

WELL

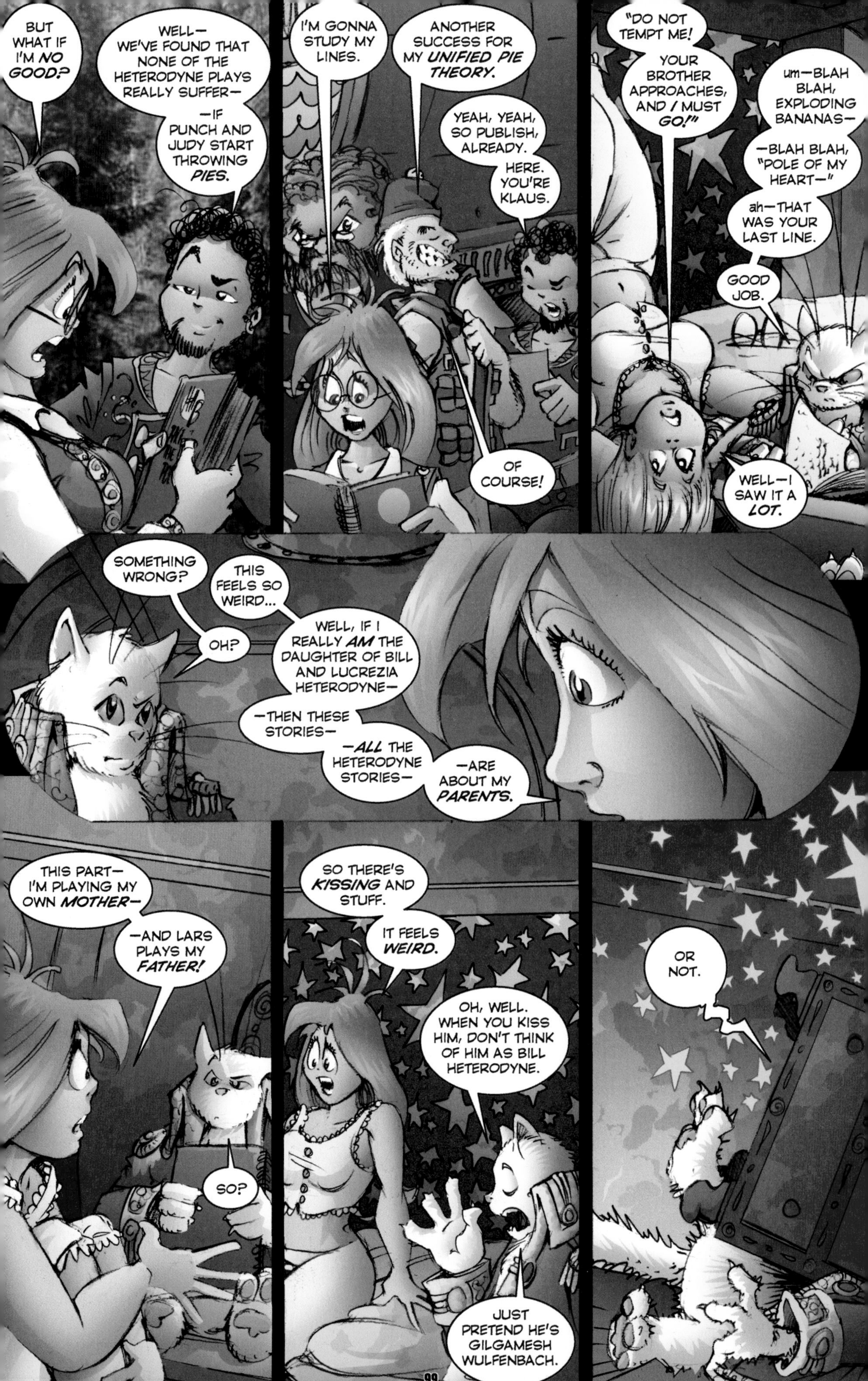
BUT WHAT IF I'M NO GOOD?
WELL— WE'VE FOUND THAT NONE OF THE HETERODYNE PLAYS REALLY SUFFER—
—IF PUNCH AND JUDY START THROWING PIES.
I'M GONNA STUDY MY LINES.
ANOTHER SUCCESS FOR MY UNIFIED PIE THEORY.
YEAH, YEAH, SO PUBLISH, ALREADY.
HERE. YOU'RE KLAUS.
OF COURSE!
"DO NOT TEMPT ME!
YOUR BROTHER APPROACHES, AND I MUST GO!"
um—BLAH BLAH, EXPLODING BANANAS—
—BLAH BLAH, "POLE OF MY HEART—"
ah—THAT WAS YOUR LAST LINE.
GOOD JOB.
WELL—I SAW IT A LOT.
SOMETHING WRONG?
THIS FEELS SO WEIRD...
OH?
WELL, IF I REALLY AM THE DAUGHTER OF BILL AND LUCREZIA HETERODYNE—
—THEN THESE STORIES—
—ALL THE HETERODYNE STORIES—
—ARE ABOUT MY PARENTS.
THIS PART— I'M PLAYING MY OWN MOTHER—
—AND LARS PLAYS MY FATHER!
SO?
SO THERE'S KISSING AND STUFF.
IT FEELS WEIRD.
OH, WELL. WHEN YOU KISS HIM, DON'T THINK OF HIM AS BILL HETERODYNE.
JUST PRETEND HE'S GILGAMESH WULFENBACH.
OR NOT.

A FEW DAYS LATER, IN THE TOWN OF ZUMZUM—

SHE'S GUNNA *KEEL* US, HYU KNOW.

HY *KNOW,* HY *KNOW.*

HO! VE SHOULD GET OFF SO *EASY.*

HYU GOTS *THAT* RIGHT.

SHE CAN BE *VERY* UNREASONABLE.

HEY! VAIT A MINUTE!

MAYBE VE GETS *LUCKY!*

MEBBE VE BE *DEAD* BY THE TIME SHE GETS HERE!

OOH! HADN'T THOUGHT OF *THAT!*

IZ YOU CRAZY? DEN VE *REALLY* BE IN TROUBLE!

HO— COMPANY!

ARE YOU *INSANE?* WE CAN'T PERFORM *HERE!*

I *KNOW* SIR— I *TRIED.*

BUT ALL ENTERTAINM *HAS* TO BE THE *TOW. SQUARE*

PERFORMING NEXT TO CORPSES IS DISRESPECTFUL—

—AND UNHYGIENIC!

AH—WELL, IF *THAT'S* THE ONLY PROBLEM—

100

WHAT DID THEY *DO?*

BE JÄGERMONSTERS AND GET *CAPTURED,* WHAT ELSE?

OH. BUT—

—WON'T THE BARON BE *UPSET?*

THE BARON DON'T CARE ABOUT *US,* MISS.

SERGEANT ZULI, AT YOUR SERVICE.

IT'S A *RARE* EVENT WHEN WE SEE THE BARON'S PATROL SHIPS OVERHEAD.

WE'RE TOO SMALL AND OUT-OF-THE-WAY HERE.

PLUS, THESE ONES WEREN'T EVEN WEARING HIS BADGE.

THESE ARE *WILD* JÄGERS.

AND TO THEM WITH LONG MEMORIES—

—THEM WHAT REMEMBERS THE HETERODYNES—

—THAT MAKES THEM *FAIR GAME.*

BLESS YOU, MISS. OF COURSE THEY WERE THE *GOOD* ONES.

I MEAN *BEFORE* THEM.

THE *HETERODYNES!* BUT BILL AND BARRY—

THE *OLD* HETERODYNES.

"MURDERIN' DEVILS, EVERY ONE—"

"—AND THE JÄGERS RODE WITH THEM—"

"—KILLIN' FOR SPORT AND LAYING WASTE WHEREVER THEY WENT."

THAT'S WHAT THE OLD FOLKS REMEMBER.

TO THEM, THIS IS JUST THE WHEEL OF JUSTICE GRINDING *SLOW* BUT *FINE.*

WELL, GOOD DAY, LADIES.

HEY!

SMAK!

I...I HADN'T... REALLY *THOUGHT* ABOUT IT.

NOT LIKE *THAT.*

WELL, YEAH. THE HETERODYNE BOYS REALLY REDEEMED THE FAMILY.

BUT PEOPLE STILL SCARE THEIR KIDS WITH STORIES ABOUT THE JÄGERS.

NOW, THAT'S *CREEPY.*

WHAT?

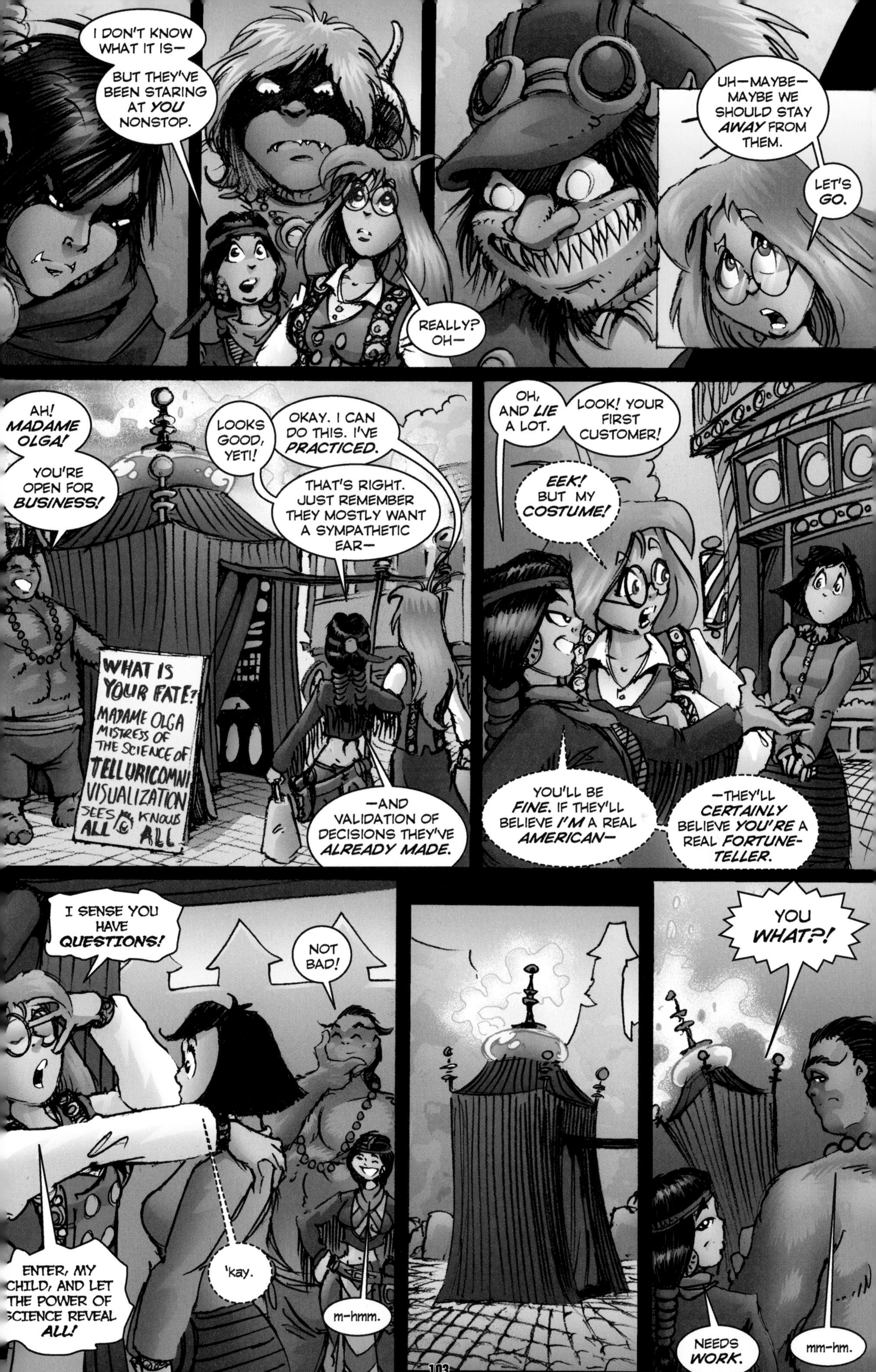
I DON'T KNOW WHAT IT IS—
BUT THEY'VE BEEN STARING AT YOU NONSTOP.
REALLY? OH—
UH—MAYBE—MAYBE WE SHOULD STAY AWAY FROM THEM.
LET'S GO.
AH! MADAME OLGA!
YOU'RE OPEN FOR BUSINESS!
LOOKS GOOD, YETI!
OKAY. I CAN DO THIS. I'VE PRACTICED.
THAT'S RIGHT. JUST REMEMBER THEY MOSTLY WANT A SYMPATHETIC EAR—
WHAT IS YOUR FATE?
MADAME OLGA MISTRESS OF THE SCIENCE OF TELLURICOMNI VISUALIZATION
SEES ALL KNOWS ALL
—AND VALIDATION OF DECISIONS THEY'VE ALREADY MADE.
OH, AND LIE A LOT.
LOOK! YOUR FIRST CUSTOMER!
EEK! BUT MY COSTUME!
YOU'LL BE FINE. IF THEY'LL BELIEVE I'M A REAL AMERICAN—
—THEY'LL CERTAINLY BELIEVE YOU'RE A REAL FORTUNE-TELLER.
I SENSE YOU HAVE QUESTIONS!
NOT BAD!
ENTER, MY CHILD, AND LET THE POWER OF SCIENCE REVEAL ALL!
'kay.
m-hmm.
YOU WHAT?!
NEEDS WORK.
mm-hm.

SOON—

YOU'RE ALMOST ON! *NERVOUS?*

RELAX! IF YOU MESS UP WE'LL COVER FOR YOU!

DADDY! HERE'S MORE *PIES!*

ONLY BECAUSE PEOPLE KEEP ASKING ME THAT!

OKAY. *NOW* I'M NERVOUS.

NO NO *NO!* YOU'RE *LUCREZIA MONGFISH!*

YOU'RE *MAD!* YOU'RE *BAD!* YOU'RE *DANGEROUS!*

YES! YES! "I THINK TOO MUCH— —THEREFORE I AM MAD!" *GRR!*

"I PRAY THE MISTRESS IS IN A GOOD MOOD—"

THAT'S YOUR CUE! GO!

OF *COURSE* I AM!

IT IS A *GLORIOUS* DAY FOR—

GAK!

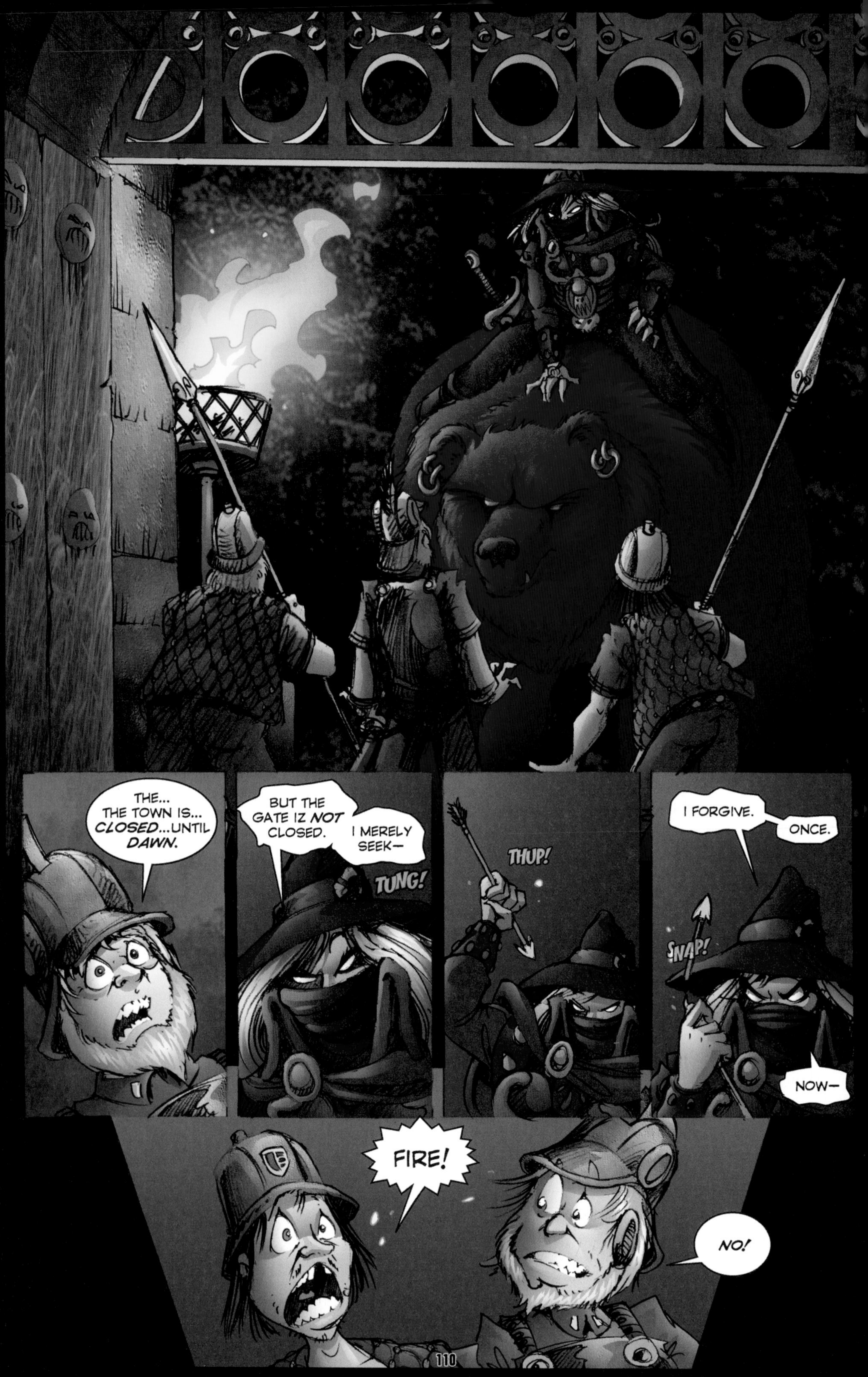

THE... THE TOWN IS... CLOSED...UNTIL DAWN.
BUT THE GATE IZ NOT CLOSED.
I MERELY SEEK—
TUNG!
THUP!
I FORGIVE.
ONCE.
SNAP!
NOW—
FIRE!
NO!

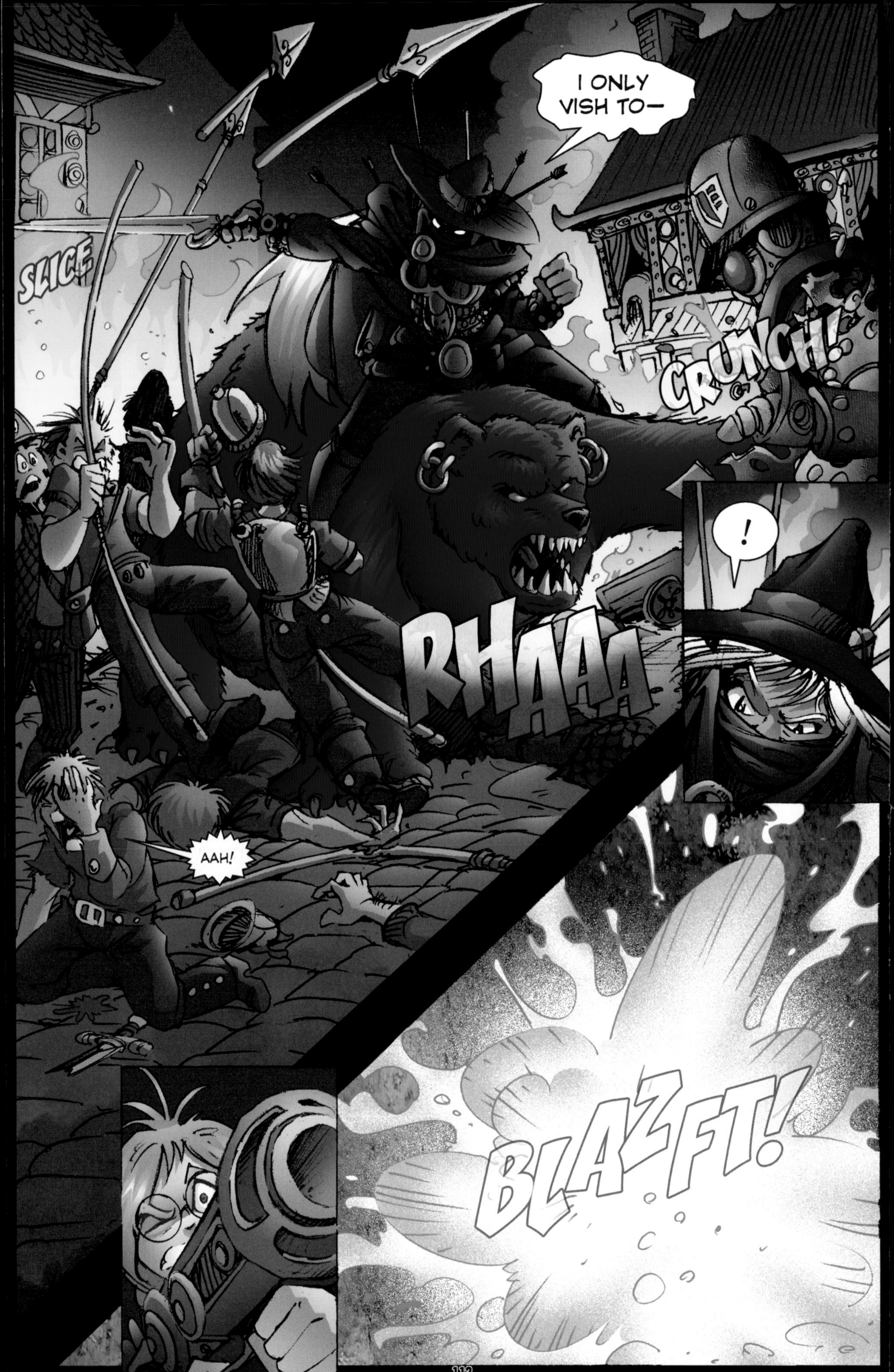
I ONLY VISH TO—
SLICE
CRUNCH!
RHAAA
AAH!
!
BLAZFT!

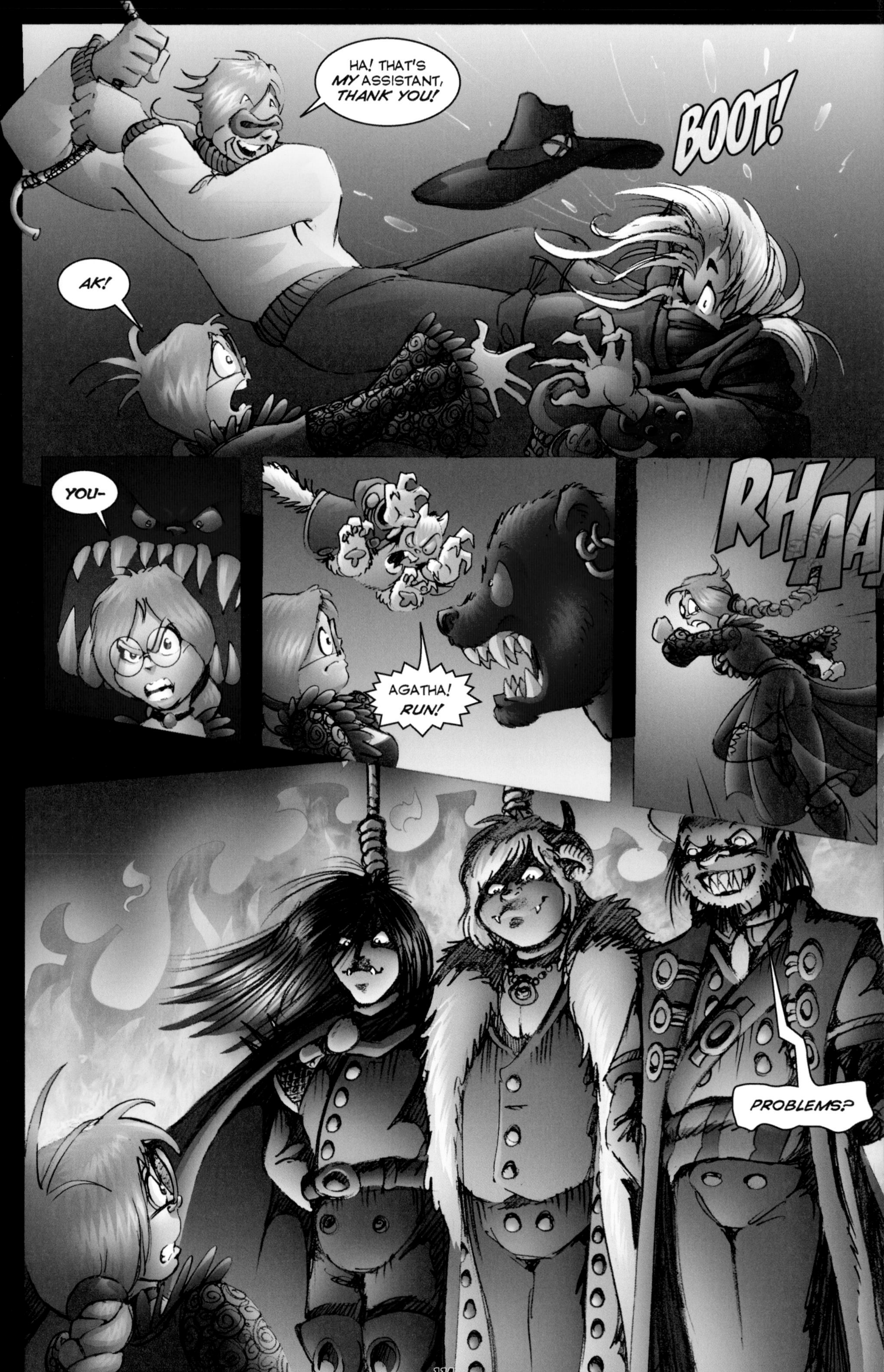

HA! THAT'S MY ASSISTANT, THANK YOU!
BOOT!
AK!
YOU-
AGATHA! RUN!
RHAA
PROBLEMS?

TO BE CONTINUED IN: GIRL GENIUS® Book FIVE:

AGATHA HETERODYNE & THE CLOCKWORK PRINCESS

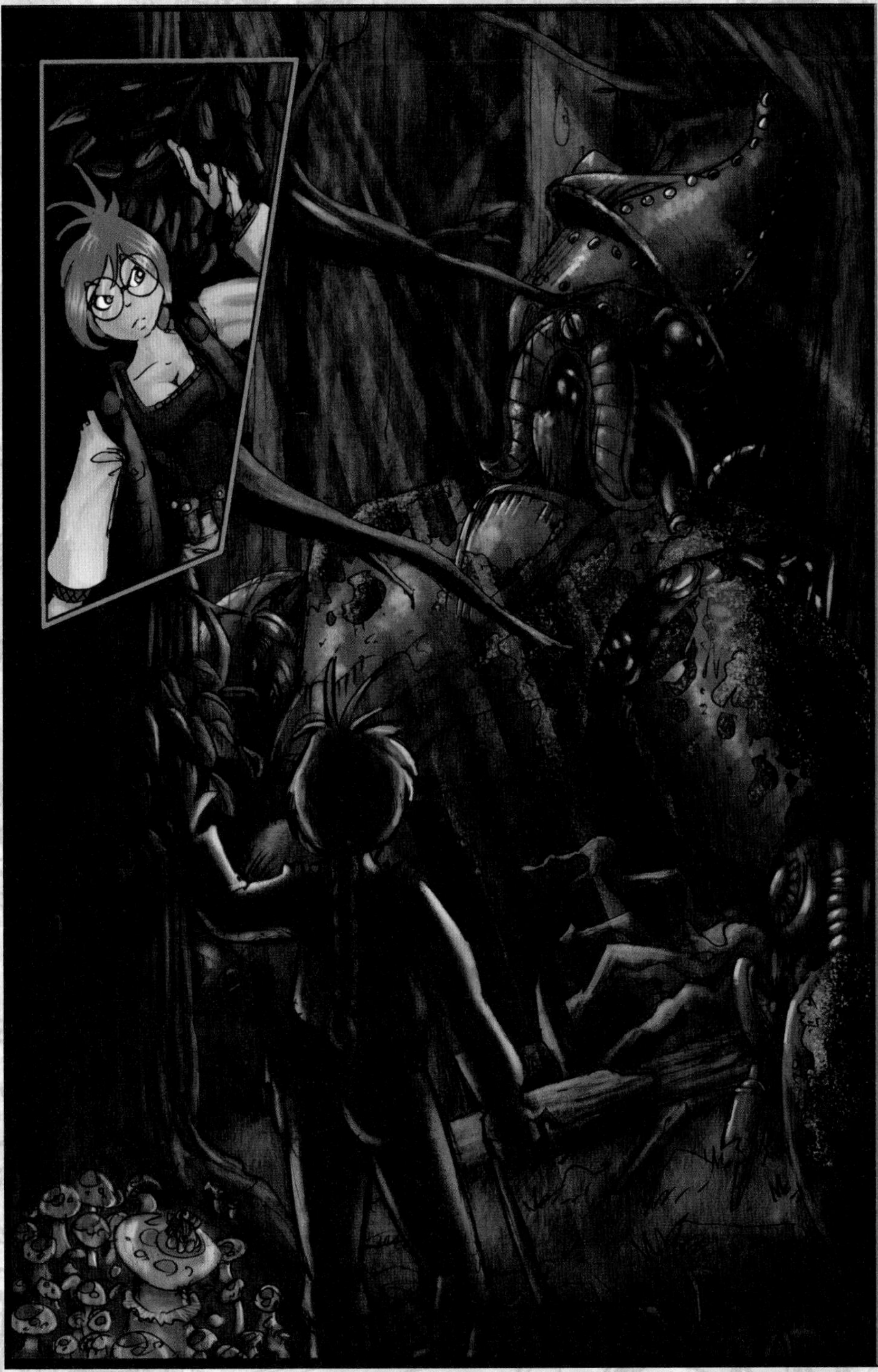

READ NEW COMICS THREE TIMES A WEEK AT:

WWW.GIRLGENIUS.NET

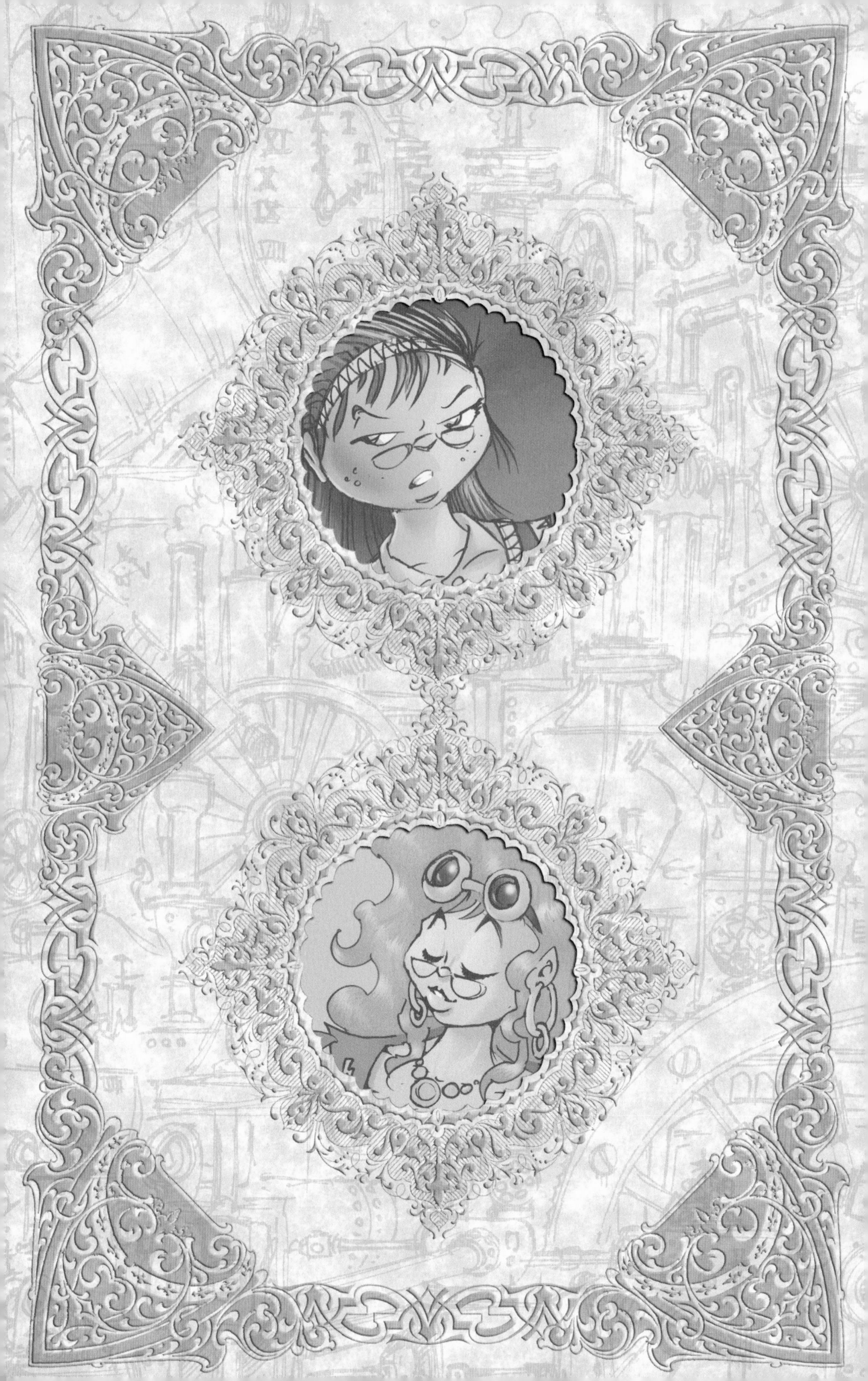

WANT TO HEAR A STORY?

YEAH! A HETERODYNE BOYS STORY!

BUT TELL IT *RIGHT*, MARY!

DON'T MESS IT UP THIS TIME.

OKAY, HOW ABOUT...

Fan Fiction

"*THE TURBINES OF ATLANTIS?*"

Story:
Chaenon K. Garrity

Pictures:
Phil Foglio

Colors:
Cheyenne Wright

"I KNOW *TURBINES OF ATLANTIS!*"

"THAT'S A GOOD ONE!"

BILL & BARRY HETERODYNE

"GLAD YOU APPROVE.

SO THE HETERODYNE BOYS WERE CROSSING THE ATLANTIC,

ON THEIR WAY TO SHUT DOWN THE MAD PERFUMERIES OF HAITI..."

THE *WAVE-WALKER* WORKS EVEN BETTER THAN WE PLANNED!

WE'LL BE PUTTING THAT ARMY OF *SCENT ZOMBIES* TO REST BY SUPPER!

BILL! *LOOK!*

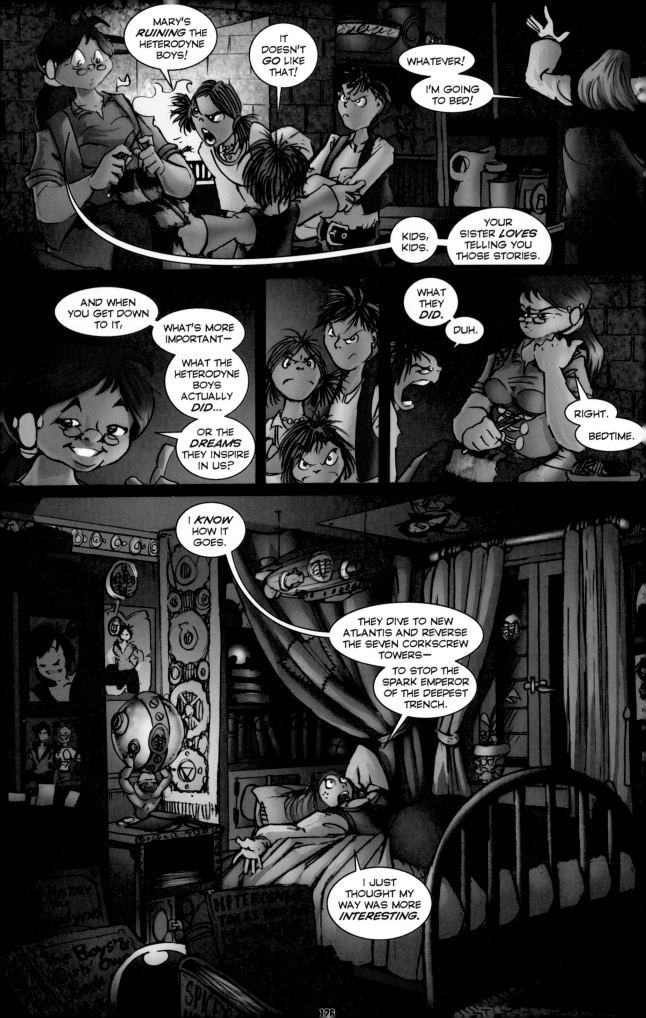

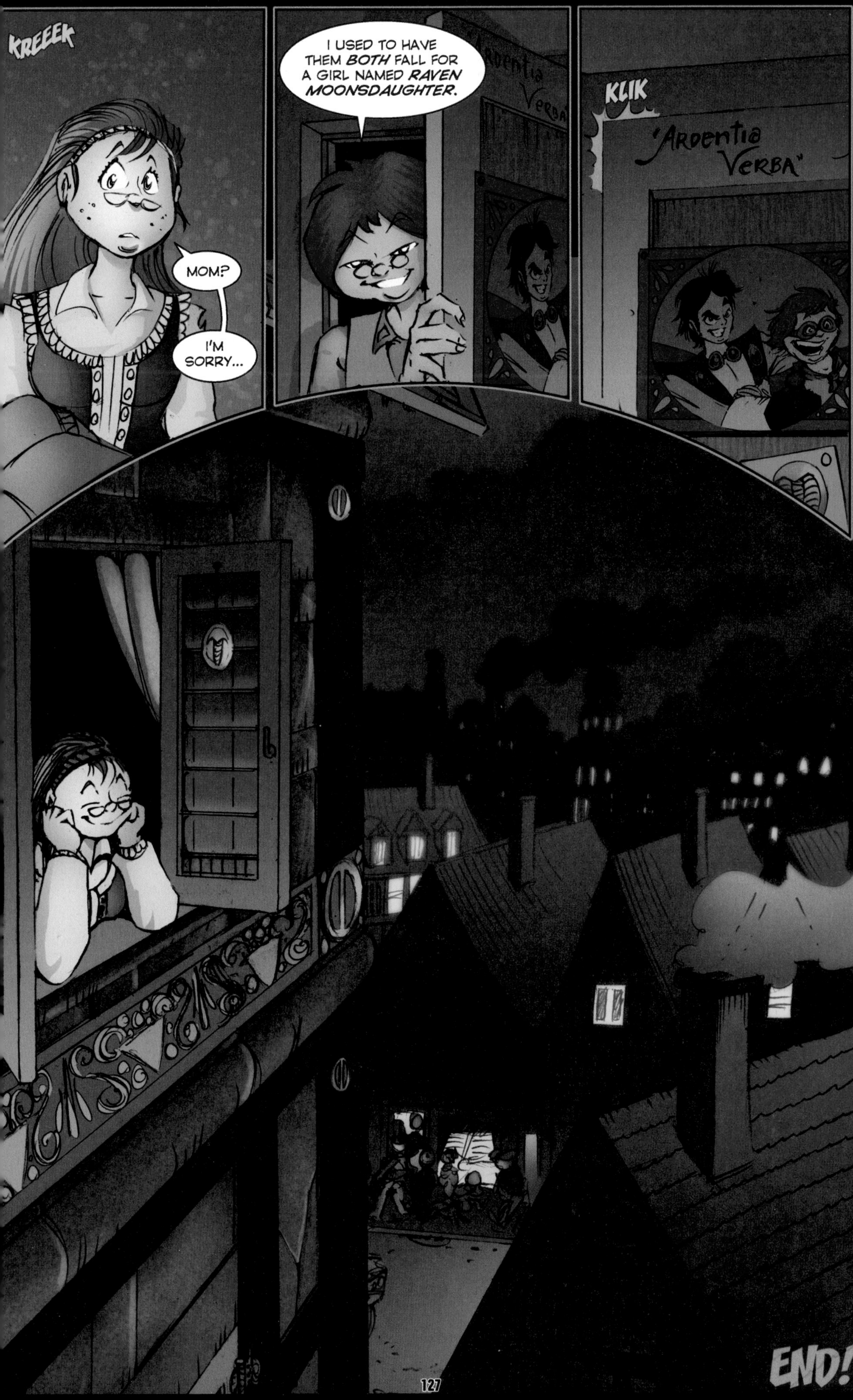
KREEEK
MOM?
I'M SORRY...
I USED TO HAVE THEM BOTH FALL FOR A GIRL NAMED RAVEN MOONSDAUGHTER.
KLIK
"ARDENTIA VERBA"
END!